MEND IT!

A complete guide to clothes repair.

Maureen Goldsworthy

If you've ever torn a favorite suit, ripped an expensive blouse, or if your children find inventive ways to put holes in their clothes, you know that the cost of professional repair often exceeds the original cost of the garment. And with inflation eating all of us out of house and home, more and more folks are turning worn collars and cuffs to save money. If you want to mend it, *whatever it is*, you'll be thankful for this manual, the comprehensive guide to clothes repair.

The author explains darning by hand and machine, patching, repairing knitted fabrics whether hand or warp knitted or double jersey, mending with adhesives, repairs to special fabrics such as velvet, towelling, corduroy, lace, embroidery, rubberized fabric, leather, suede, or fur (including fake fur).

Here's all you need to know about split seams, buttons and buttonholes, jacket cuffs, pockets, re-seating trousers, waistbands, shirt collars and cuffs, zippers, and worn armholes as well as camouflaging, reinforcing, panel replacement, relining, and more. The techniques are illustrated with over 230 foolproof detailed line diagrams and 25 photos.

(Continued on back flap)

How to Paint Anything:
The Complete Guide to Painting and Refinishing
by Hubbard Cobb

MEND IT!

a complete guide to clothes repair

MEND IT!
a complete guide to clothes repair

Maureen Goldsworthy

STEIN AND DAY/*Publishers*/New York

First published in the United States of America in 1980
by Stein & Day/*Publishers*

Copyright © 1979 by Maureen Goldsworthy

Printed in the United States of America
Stein and Day/*Publishers*/Scarborough House
Briarcliff Manor, N.Y. 10510

Library of Congress Cataloging in Publication Data
Goldsworthy, Maureen.
  Mend it!

  1.   Clothing and dress — Repairing.   2.   Needlework.
I.   Title.
TT720.G65   1980   646.2   79-3709
ISBN 0-8128-2695-7
ISBN 0-8128-6046-2 pbk.

Acknowledgment

The author is greatly indebted to Mrs. Vera Hodgkiss and Mrs. Peggy Eden, of Messrs. Sketchley Ltd., for their kindness in allowing her to study, under their skilled guidance, the methods used in the garment repair trade. She is most grateful to Mrs. Pat Hayden for information on technical terms and trade names used in the United States, to Mr Wilfred Lawson for his helpful criticism and to Mr Robert Saunders of Wright Photography for the photographic illustrations.

For
A.E.C.H.

Contents

Note

Throughout the book, shading indicates the
right side of fabric, as in commercial dress
patterns.

'As invisible as possible . . .'

A cigarette burn on a good skirt – a tear in a new pair of pants – ripped buttonholes or worn front edges on a man's jacket – a hole at the elbow of a favourite sweater – none of these is any reason for abandoning an expensive garment to oblivion or the next jumble sale. Mend it! Not perhaps with an eye-catching darn or a thumping great patch, but with one of the many methods that will make a nearly or completely invisible repair, often in considerably less time.

The cost of replacement can now be so high that a repair taking an hour or two makes excellent sense. One need not be an experienced needlewoman to undertake most of the repairs shown in this book.

The standard mending techniques were evolved at a time when the labour of semp-stresses was cheap and when most repairs, on layer after layer of undergarments, were designed to be strong rather than unobtrusive. In an early manual for student teachers of needlework, Amy K. Smith recommends a particularly conspicuous type of patch for 'that portion of the bodice against which the whalebone of the corset or dress bodice rubs.'

Fortunately, no such considerations need trouble us now. Indeed, the whole pattern of clothes repair has changed. With the advent of man-made fibres, underwear rarely needs mending before the whole garment is ready to be scrapped: its replacement will be relatively cheap. Now, it is the appallingly expensive suit, jacket or skirt that will be worth your time and trouble to repair and, moreover, to repair meticulously and invisibly.

Miss Smith, evidently one of those typically practical and forward-looking Victorians, roundly condemns on this score some con-temporary methods of repair. 'This process involves a deal more darning than there is any necessity for, consequently takes longer to darn, is no more effectual, and renders a tear on dress material clumsy, as it makes much of what is really very little, and which should be as invisible as possible.' Following her lead, the author takes this as the first criterion of good mending.

Next in importance is time. Nowadays the time to spare for looking after our clothes is as restricted as were our great-grandmothers' waists in their whalebone stays. There is little point in spending time on work that can be simplified by modern sewing machines. Machine-worked darns and patches are almost always preferable to hand-worked ones; as well as being less visible, they are usually stronger. Man-made fibres and new types of fabric, such as the stretchable knits, both present problems which call for new – and sometimes surprisingly simple – methods of repair. The various classes of knitted fabrics are here treated separately and in some detail.

The specialized tailoring repair methods are perhaps the most valuable of all. Those most commonly needed are fully described in the last section of the book.

MEND IT!

a complete guide to clothes repair

DARNING

Darning

Darning may be defined as the introduction of new threads to reinforce those that are worn, or to replace those that are broken. This definition covers repairs to thin places, tears and holes. The verb 'to darn' is related to the Middle Dutch *dernen*, meaning to stop up a hole in a dyke. This has more than linguistic interest: the parallel is plain. A precautionary darn over worn fabric, before a hole has actually appeared, is quicker and easier to work, gives a better result and will be far less visible.

Darning can be worked on any fabric, woven or knitted, though the technique is varied according to the weight, substance and texture of the fabric. Some warp-knit and double-knit fabrics, especially in man-made fibres, have the firmness of woven fabrics; they are better treated as such, and darned with the method normally used for a woven fabric of similar handle.

The versatility of swing-needle sewing machines and the development of fine polyester threads have combined to extend the usefulness of machine-darning. In most cases nowadays, a machine-worked darn would be preferable to a hand-worked one. They are treated here in separate sections.

All darns have three elements in common:
1. The first set of mending strands must be laid parallel to the warp threads of the fabric or, in the case of knitted fabrics, parallel to the wale of the knit. The stronger threads, in fact, should be replaced first in order to retain the shape of the damaged fabric.
2. The darn should be large enough to cover any thin area round the actual hole, so that a firm darn is not set into a weakened surround which would tend to tear at the edge of the darn. Worn parts round a hole, however, are less common with the stronger man-made fibres than with natural fibres such as wool or cotton, so in general, darns may nowadays be much smaller and therefore less conspicuous than formerly.
3. The shape of the darn must be such that the mending strands do not place strain on any single warp or weft thread of the fabric. Darns therefore should not be square in outline. *Figure 1* shows the shapes commonly used.

The threads used for darning should be matched as closely as possible to the colour, thickness and texture of the fabric. It is not always possible – or even desirable – to match the fibre from which the garment was made. So a woollen sweater could be mended with a wool-nylon thread, which would give better wear and less shrinkage. A cotton or rayon fabric could be darned with a polyester machine-darning or machine-embroidery thread, or with a stranded embroidery cotton, whichever best matches the sheen and texture of the fabric. But, conversely, threads of natural fibre are not suitable for mending synthetic fabrics because they are unlikely to be as strong and because they may be liable to shrinkage. Where the threads of the fabric itself are coarse enough to handle, these are the best of all for hand-darning; take them from the facings or seam-turnings of the garment, using the warp and weft threads in their proper direction in the darn. This would, however, be impracticable in a light-weight, finely-woven fabric.

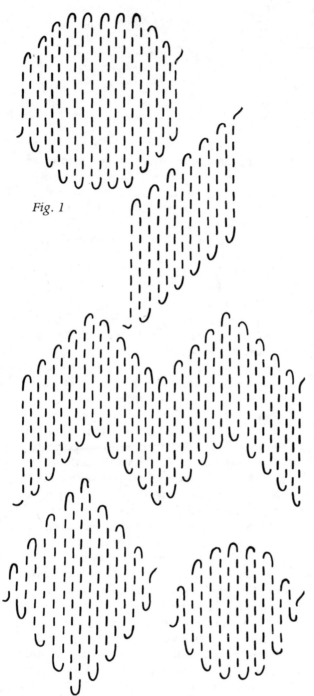

Fig. 1

Darning by hand

The Plain Darn

Use a darning needle, which will be long enough to pick up the stitches along the whole length of the darn, before pulling the thread through.

1. On the wrong side, begin at the left of the area to be darned, two or three stitches away from the hole or thin place. Pick up and pass over equal groups of weft threads, taking about three stitches to the centimetre (eight to the inch). There is no merit in finer darning than will produce a closely-woven web over the hole. However, *Figure 2* shows a darn which takes up and passes over a single thread; if the weave is coarse enough, this gives the least conspicuous result.

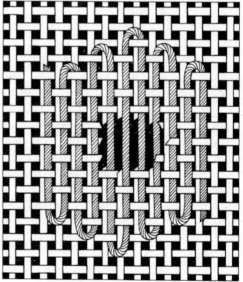

Fig. 2

2. Bearing in mind the final shape of the darn, begin each successive row one stitch higher, and end one stitch lower. At the end of each stranding, leave a very small loop to allow movement in the finished darn, and to avoid strain on the threads of the fabric. The strands should be placed almost touching each other, so that the hole itself will be fully filled.

3. Begin the weft stranding by taking up both a warpwise mending thread and its corresponding thread in the body of the fabric. The weft stranding, in fact, goes right through the fabric. Take up and pass over the threads alternately, as shown in *Figure 3*, being careful to weave accurately over the hole itself. No finishing-off is necessary.

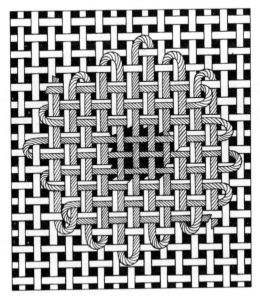

Fig. 3

4. Press the darn to settle in the strandings.

The Thin-Place Darn
This is worked in the same way as the hole darn, except that it would not usually be necessary to lay any weftwise strandings. Be sure the darn extends far enough to be anchored safely into unworn fabric.

The Twill Darn
If the weave is sufficiently coarse for the threads to be seen clearly, a twill darn should be made, following the pattern of the weave. Take up and pass over the same number of threads as in the fabric. The example in *Figure 4* shows a twill in which the warp threads pass under and over two weft threads, moving up one for the return journey. The weft threads follow the same pattern.

Fig. 4

The Damask Darn
Many other weaving patterns can be imitated in darning. This is of less importance now than in the last century, when table linens in damask weaves were exquisitely and invisibly darned to match the pattern. Examples of two weaves used in dress fabrics are shown here. A hopsack weave, with threads woven in pairs,

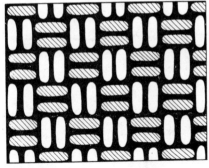

Fig 5

Fig. 6

17

is shown in *Figure 5*. A herringbone weave, of which there are many variations, is shown in *Figure 6*; the one illustrated is the simplest, where both warp and weft take up and pass over two threads. These darns can be worked in pattern over small holes in tweeds.

The Tear Darn

A tear caused by catching the fabric on a nail or sharp point – traditionally known as a *hedge-tear* – will have clean edges along the warp and weft of the fabric; there will not usually be any wear in the surrounding area, so the darn may be kept very narrow.

1. On the wrong side, draw the edges together with fishbone or lacing stitch. *Figure 7*. This holds the fabric firmly and makes for easier darning.

2. Beginning not more than 1cm (⅜in") from the tear, lay the warp strands. *Figure 8*. Alternately pick up and pass over the edge of the tear.

3. Lay the weft strands along the other arm of the tear. The small square at the point is the only part over which both strandings are worked. *Figure 9*. Leave the fishbone-stitching in place; it should be unnoticeable, and helps to strengthen the repair.

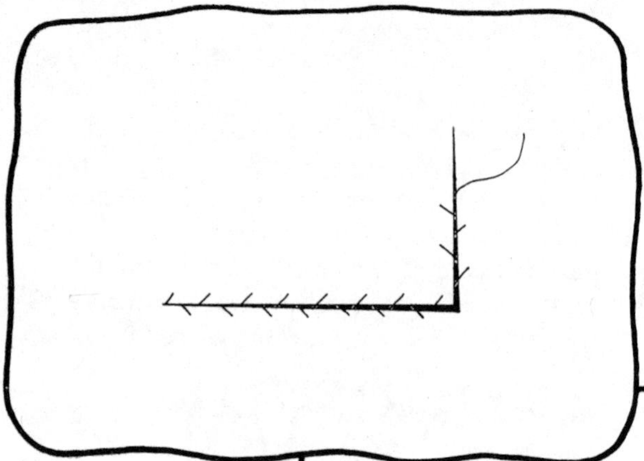

Fig. 7

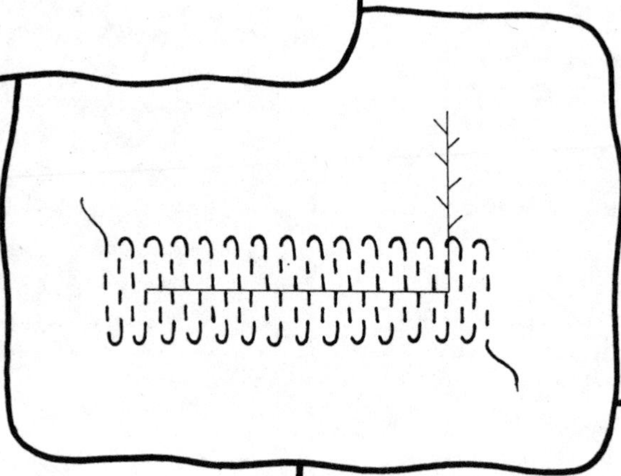

Fig. 8

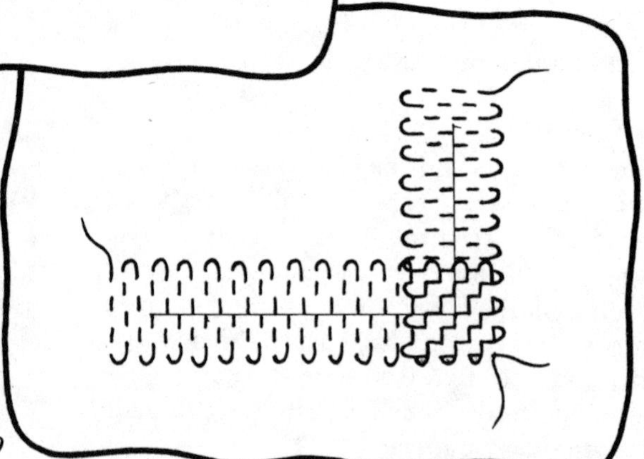

Fig. 9

The Cross-Cut Darn

In a clean cut at any angle across the weave, both warp and weft threads will have been broken, so this repair needs to be handled gently to prevent stretching and fraying. It is not usually advisable, therefore, to work a row of fishbone-stitch between the edges.

The traditional shape of the darn is shown in *Figure 10*. This consists of two rhomboids, although at first sight it appears to be a pair of overlapping triangles.

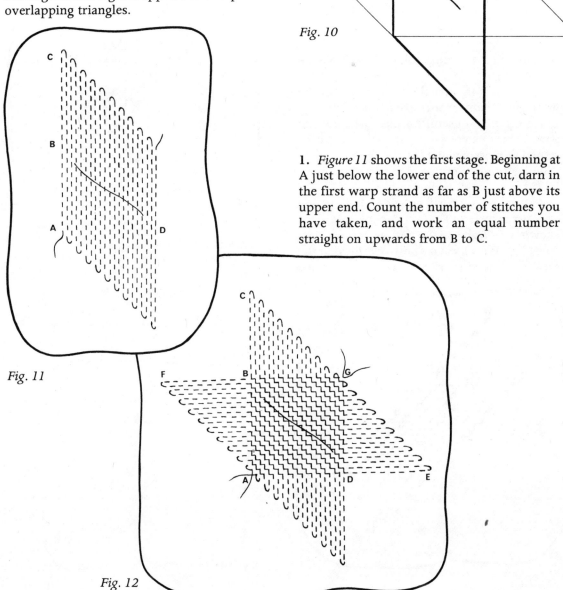

Fig. 10

Fig. 11

Fig. 12

1. *Figure 11* shows the first stage. Beginning at A just below the lower end of the cut, darn in the first warp strand as far as B just above its upper end. Count the number of stitches you have taken, and work an equal number straight on upwards from B to C.

19

2. Work the rest of the warp strandings, starting one stitch lower on each journey, and alternately taking up and passing over the edge of the cut. The width of the darn from A to D should measure the same as the height from A to B.

3. Work the weft strandings in the same way. *Figure 12*. Begin at A, the same point as the warp strandings. Work across to D, then take an equal number of stitches on to E.

4. Continue the rows, reducing a stitch at the right and adding a stitch at the left on each journey. The last strand will be laid from F to G, finishing at the same point as the last warp thread.

Now this is the strictly correct form of the darn, given here for the sake of completeness, but it serves no useful purpose whatever to work this extensive and elaborate construction, most of which will be merely an eye-catching addition of thread to perfectly sound fabric.

Always, a good repair should be both strong and unobtrusive. The version of this darn shown in *Figure 13* is just as strong, less conspicuous (as it covers only one-third of the area) and much quicker to work. The warp strandings are laid from A to B, ending at C – D. The weft strandings begin at E – F and finish at G – H.

An even simpler but just as satisfactory shape is shown in *Figure 14*.

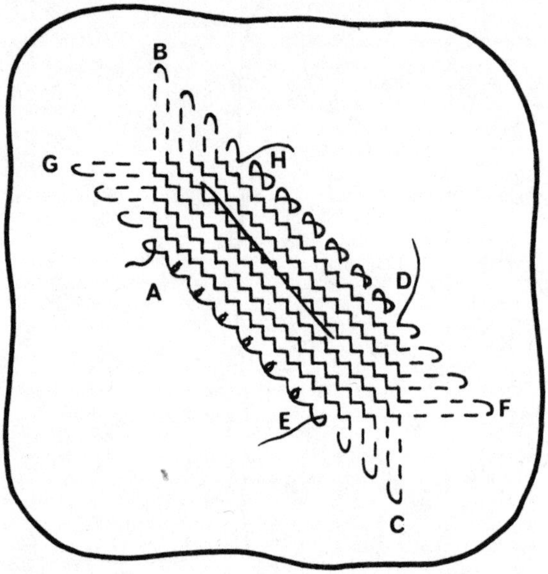

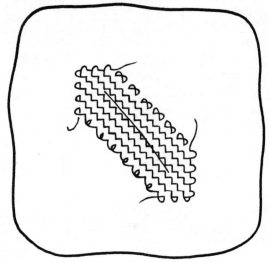

Fig. 14

The 'Invisible' Darn

This repair is possible only where two torn edges exactly fit each other, with no threads missing. It is really a pared-down version of the Cross-Cut Darn, and can be quite inconspicuous. Although it is not totally invisible, the traditional name is retained.

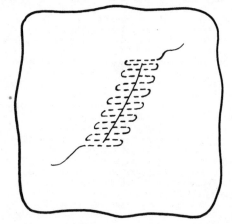

Fig. 15

Fig. 13

1. Lightly press the tear, bringing the edges together and making sure that no loose thread ends show on the right side.

2. Tack the tear, wrong side up, over a piece of paper to hold the edges together while you darn.

3. Use a thread of the same fabric and the finest crewel needle into which it will go. On the wrong side, as shown in *Figure 15*, darn across the tear in one direction only – either warpwise or weftwise, whichever direction will better hold the edges together. Only four stitches should be taken on each journey – two into each edge. As you work across the tear, pick any loose thread end through to the wrong side with the point of the needle.

4. Remove the tacking and paper and press.

The Fine-Drawn Cut Darn

This darn is suitable for repairing cuts on thick fabrics, such as coatings. It can be quite invisible, particularly if there is any slight surface nap.

Use the finest matching polyester or silk thread, or a thread of the fabric (if fine enough), in a No. 10 crewel needle.

Work from the wrong side, starting with a knot 3mm ($\frac{1}{8}$in) away from the cut. Make a slanting stitch, as in *Figure 16*, but take the needle only half-way through the thickness of the stuff, and bring it out on the wrong side again. Work these stitches 3mm ($\frac{1}{8}$in) apart, first from one side and then from the other side of the cut. With the point of the needle, lift any loose ends through to the wrong side.

There is no need to leave loops, but do not pull up the thread tightly. No stitch should penetrate to the right side of the fabric. If the cut is longer than about 3cm (1in), it is advisable first to baste the edges loosely together.

When the repair is complete, smooth over the nap with your finger, and press with steam right side down on an unpadded board.

This repair used to be worked with hair; indeed, hair is still occasionally used by some industrial repairers. On the most respectable authority,* red or white hairs are said to be stronger than other colours. But hair is awkward and springy to handle, and it must be long enough to knot double into the needle. Before the introduction of man-made fibres, no thread of the same fineness had the tensile strength of hair: now however fine polyester threads are both stronger and preferable.

Darning by machine

Wherever it is possible, a machine-worked darn is preferable to a hand-worked one. It will be stronger and almost always less noticeable.

In machine darning the fabric is moved freely forwards, backwards or sideways. It is neither held down by the presser-foot nor drawn through the machine by the teeth of the feed-dog. Imagine the needle as a fixed pencil with which, by moving the work about underneath it, you can draw straight or curved lines in any direction. The length and direction of the stitches are determined solely by the pace at which you move the fabric, longer stitches being produced if it is moved at speed, and shorter stitches if it is moved slowly. The machine itself should be run uniformly fast.

Some makes of machine have a special darning foot which applies only momentary pressure to the fabric as each stitch is made;

---

*Thérèse de Dillmont, whose superb *Encyclopedia of Needlework* (first published in English in 1890) remains the most valuable of reference books.

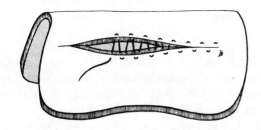

Fig. 16

with other machines no foot at all is used for darning. For your own machine, consult the instruction booklet.

As there is no pressure to hold the work flat, it must be kept stretched taut by other means, or the stitches will be formed unevenly and the fabric become puckered – even snarled into the machine under the needle. With a darning foot, it may be enough to hold the fabric stretched tightly under your fingers as you move it. Without a darning foot, it is essential to put the work into embroidery hoops. Even then, for a successful result, it must be drum-tight; it should be resonant if you flick your finger-nail against it. If you are mending a fine fabric that might slip and lose its tension, you should first bind the inner hoop with tape, as shown in *Figure 17*.

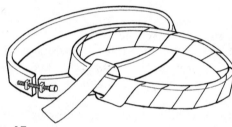

Fig. 17

For some heavier fabrics, if only a back-and-forth darn is needed, you can use the normal presser-foot and normal pressure. Then, of course, the work must be turned at the end of each row. This is a better method than using the reverse stitch where the presser-foot will obscure your view.

The choice of thread depends, of course, on the fabric you are mending – the heavier the material, the coarser the thread can be. But in general a fine matt-surfaced machine-darning thread will blend best with the surrounding fabric. The size of the machine needle used also depends on the weight of the fabric, as in any other machining.

To begin darning, prepare the machine as follows:

1. Slightly loosen the tension on the needle-thread.

2. Remove the presser-foot and, if necessary on your machine, replace it with the darning foot.

3. Drop the feed-dog so that the teeth become inoperative. (In some machines, a special darning plate is fitted instead.)

4. Set a straight stitch. The stitch-length setting is immaterial.

5. With a free-arm machine, slot in the table extension to make a wide, flat surface for the embroidery frame.

Now you are ready to darn. Place the work into the embroidery hoops, with the area to be darned in the centre. The fabric must go *under* the inner hoop and *over* the outer one, so that it is flat against the needle-plate and supported by it. *Figure 18*. Make sure that the presser-bar behind the needle is lowered, or the stitches will not form properly.

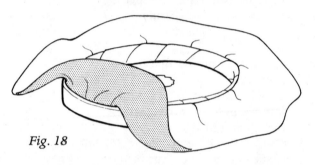

Fig. 18

Lower the needle into the work, and bring up the end of the bobbin thread. Holding both thread ends to one side, work a couple of stitches at the same point, to anchor the threads, and then cut off the ends. No loose thread must ever be left under the work, or it will tangle.

The Thin-Place Darn

For reinforcing a thin place, it is usually enough to work close rows of machining in one direction only, as shown in *Figure 19*. Hold the hoop with both hands. Move it in any direction, but do not turn it like a steering-wheel; keep your hands always at the sides. There is no reason for the lines of stitching to be kept straight; you can work just as well in long overlapping figures-of-eight, as in *Figure 20*.

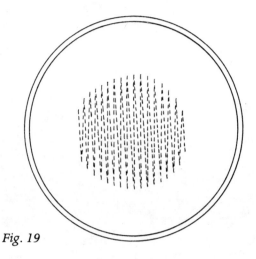

Fig. 19

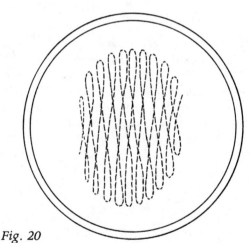

Fig. 20

The Small-Hole Darn

Where the hole is no larger than about 1.5cm ($\frac{5}{8}$in), you can darn straight across it. Indeed, much free machine embroidery makes use of stitching across a void to achieve a lace-like effect.

First, run a ring of stitches round the hole, to give firmness. Then work rows of stitching, very close together, across it. The strands, which will twist into two-ply threads over the hole, should be almost touching. Lastly, work the strandings up and down the hole. *Figure 21.* If the hole still seems too thinly covered, more strandings can be laid on top.

A woven pattern in the fabric can to some extent be imitated by the directions along which the strandings are laid.

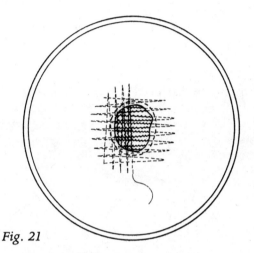

Fig. 21

The Large-Hole Darn

Although it is possible to repair larger holes by the above method, the result tends to be uneven and untidy. It is better to use a thin gauze backing to support the darn. Tarlatan or organdie are suitable for heavier fabrics, while net or tulle are better for fine ones.

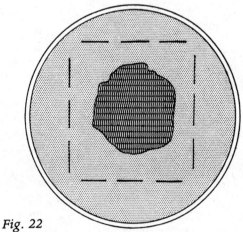

Fig. 22

Tack the supporting gauze to the wrong side of the hole. *Figure 22*. Work the darn from the right side, in the same way as before. When the darn is finished, the gauze will not be visible. Trim off the surplus close to the stitching on the wrong side.

Any sizeable darn may show up more clearly than a patch: if you have matching fabric available, you might be better advised to work one of the machine patches described on pages 39 to 44.

The Cut-Edge Darn
Where there has been damage to the edge of the fabric (admittedly a more likely occurrence in household textiles than in clothing) this can be repaired by lacing the edge tightly into embroidery hoops, as in *Figure 23*.

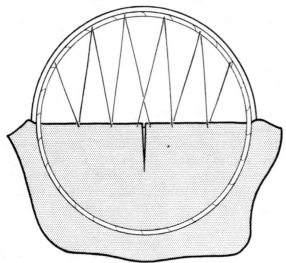

Fig. 23

First work several rows of stitching parallel and close to the edge, then fill in across the rest of the damage. Work the second set of strandings up and down over the edge. Finish off either with a few more rows along the edge, or else take the work out of the frame and make a firm edge of machine satin-stitch.

The Reinforced Cut-Edge Darn
Lay a narrow tape or ribbon along the edge of the fabric, to take the strain. Tack it in place before lacing the work into the hoops. This repair should be worked wrong-side-up as in *Figure 24*.

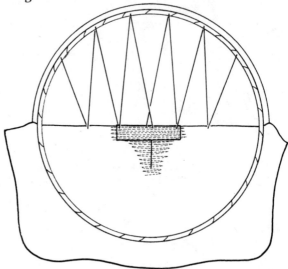

Fig. 24

The Tear Darn
If supported by a gauze backing, this darn can be very narrow and inconspicuous. Tack the backing to the wrong side and work the arms of the darn as shown in *Figure 25*. Begin at the top of one arm and work down to below the corner. Change direction and continue without a break to work the other arm. On the wrong side, trim off the gauze close to the stitching.

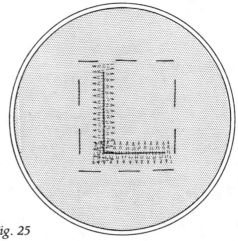

Fig. 25

The Cross-Cut Darn

If the edges of the cut are clean, it can be darned with the machine set for normal sewing. No frame is needed.

Use a gauze backing. Set the 3-step zig-zag stitch, at a short length and at its greatest width. (This stitch is shown in the seam photographed on page 115.) Work a single row of stitches, centred down the cut. This is a very simple and inconspicuous repair, sufficiently strong on a firmly-woven fabric. The wrong side is shown in Figure 26.

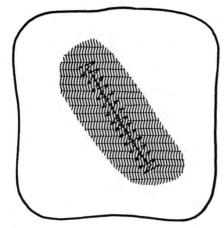

Fig. 26

PATCHING

Patching

Any patch should be both firm and nearly invisible. Some can be totally invisible. The three types traditionally set in by hand – the Felled Patch, the Oversewn Patch and the Herringboned Patch – tended to sacrifice invisibility to strength because the fabrics on which they were worked, mainly linen and flannel, were expected to have an almost indefinite life, and because washing methods were harsher than those we use now.

There are few modern fabrics on which a hand-set patch would be as little noticeable as one worked by machine, though small patches on thick or patterned materials have their uses.

A patch may be square or oblong, but its edges must be cut exactly on the straight grain. Draw threads out, if necessary, to guide you when cutting. An exception is where a patch is taken into a seam along one of its sides. For instance, a hole close to a seam in a skirt or pants might be less noticeable if the nearest side of the patch were extended into it; in this case, three sides should be cut on the straight thread of the fabric, but the fourth should correspond to the unpicked edge of the seam turning. The grain is matched to the grain of the garment.

Material for patches can usually be taken from the garment itself. Small ones can be cut from the seam turnings, inside pockets, facings, shoulder pads, waistbands or belt. A matching garment – such as the waistcoat of a man's suit – could be cannibalized for such large-scale jobs as the reseating of trousers. Unless absolutely necessary, it is better not to use the hem turning, as that would prevent your lengthening the garment later on, should fashion change.

Pieces of fabric left over from dressmaking should never be thrown out during the lifetime of the garment; even the smallest scrap might be needed for new bound buttonholes, perhaps, or for a patch. Tailors' swatches are also an excellent source of nearly-matching materials; reinforcing patches on the wrong side of the fabric need not necessarily be a true match.

Patching by hand

The Felled Patch

This is also known as the *Calico Patch*. It is used on plain fabrics where great firmness is needed.

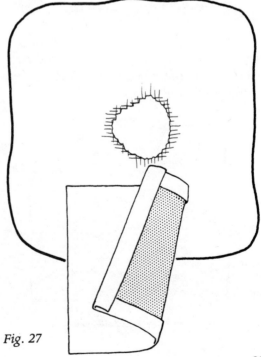

Fig. 27

1. Cut the patch large enough to cover not only the hole, but also any thin area around it, and allow 1cm ($\frac{3}{8}$in) all round for turnings. Fold the turnings to the right side of the patch, and press. *Figure 27.*

2. Place the patch wrong side up on the wrong side of the garment, exactly matching the direction of warp and weft threads. Tack in place. Fell by picking up only a thread or two of the garment, but taking a longer stitch through the fold of the patch. A stitch should fall at each corner. *Figure 28.*

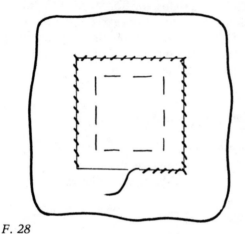

F. 28

3. Turn over to the right side. Cut away the fabric inside the patch to a width of 1.5cm ($\frac{5}{8}$in) from the stitching. *Figure 29.*

Fig. 29

4. Clip 5mm ($\frac{1}{4}$in) into each corner, fold under the raw edges, press, and fell. *Figure 30.*

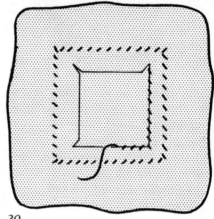

Fig. 30

The Oversewn Patch

This patch, also known as the *Print Patch*, is worked from the right side of the garment, and is therefore useful for the precise matching of a printed or checked pattern. Only one line of stitching shows on the right side, so it is less conspicuous than the Felled Patch.

1. Choose a piece of fabric that matches the part of the pattern to be cut away. This may most accurately be done by first pinning the spare fabric over the hole and then cutting out the patch. Allow 1.5cm ($\frac{5}{8}$in) turnings. Fold the turnings to the wrong side, and press. *Figure 31.*

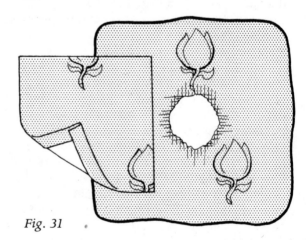

Fig. 31

2. Tack in place, matching the pattern. *Figure 32.*

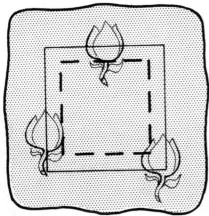

Fig. 32

3. Working from the right side, fold the garment level with one edge of the patch. Oversew the two folds together, taking up only a thread or two at each stitch. According to the fabric, you might take up to 8 stitches to the centimetre (20 to the inch). At the corner, re-fold the garment and continue along the next side.

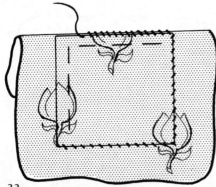

Fig. 33

4. Press, to flatten the seams.
5. The simpler and stronger way to finish this patch is to trim the worn fabric – and the patch turnings – to a width of 1cm ($\frac{3}{8}$in) and blanket-stitch the two edges together. Take care not to catch in the patch behind the turnings. *Figure 34.*

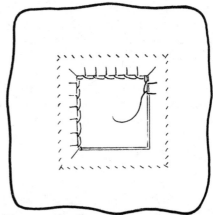

Fig. 34

6. On fabrics such as woollens, where a double thickness would be bulky, a better way is to clip the garment turnings right into each corner, mitre the patch turnings, and then press the edges apart. Finish by overcasting each edge separately. *Figure 35.*

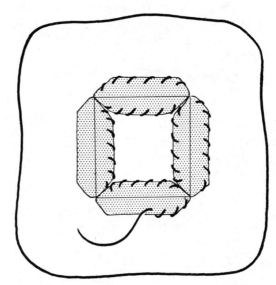

Fig. 35

The Herringboned Patch
This type of patch is for use on thick but washable fabrics. It is also known, indeed, as the *Flannel Patch* and was in Victorian times the standard method of repairing under-bodices and petticoats. It still has a limited use

31

for mending stretchable fabrics or such garments as children's pyjamas, though the machine version shown on page 56 would usually produce a neater, firmer job, certainly in less time.

The essential difference between this patch and most others is that here no turnings are made in the fabric. Both the raw edges of the patch and the raw edges of the hole are sewn flat. This avoids the bulkiness which turnings could make on a thick fabric, and also makes ironing easier.

Because there are no turnings to consider, the shape of the patch may be irregular. It would normally be cut along the warp and weft threads of the fabric into a square or oblong, but there is no reason why it should not be triangular or even round or oval. In fact, there is less strain on the garment during wear if any corners of the patch are rounded.

1. Cut the patch to the finished size needed to cover the hole and any worn part around it.

2. Matching the warp grain of the fabric, tack the patch to the garment, wrong sides up. *Figure 36.*

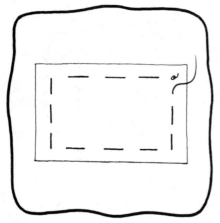

Fig. 36

3. Working from the wrong side first, herringbone-stitch round all four edges of the patch. Begin at a corner, with a backstitch. Work round the corners as shown in *Figure 37*. The stitches should be no more than 5mm ($\frac{1}{4}$in) deep, and set close together. The outer stitch

should be made in the garment fabric, just clear of the edge of the patch. The inner stitch should be taken through both thicknesses.

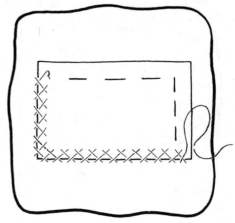

Fig. 37

4. Remove the tacking thread. Turn over to the right side. Here, the herringboning will appear as two rows of running stitches. Trim the worn area to an even 1cm ($\frac{3}{8}$in) from the inner row of stitching. Herringbone the edge as before, with the outer line of stitches picking up both thicknesses and the inner line falling just over the raw edge.

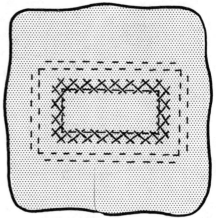

Fig. 38

5. Press. The patch should lie perfectly flat, neither pulling up the surrounding area of fabric, nor giving a blister effect by being set with too loose a tension.

The Patch for Thick Fabrics

This method, less suitable for thin materials, is very satisfactory for patching men's suitings or tweeds. Generally, the machine-set version shown on page 39 gives a better result; but very small patches are more easily manipulated by hand.

1. Cut the hole into a square or rectangle, exactly along the straight grain of the fabric. Clip diagonally into each corner to make four seam turnings 5mm ($\frac{1}{4}$in) wide. These must fold back precisely along a thread of the fabric. *Figure 39.*

2. Press the turnings back on the wrong side. *Figure 40.*

3. Pin the patching fabric under the hole, right sides up, matching the grain and any pattern. *Figure 41.*

4. Trim the patch to the size of the hole including the folded-back turnings. *Figure 42.* Unpin one side of the patch.

5. Fold back the garment at this side and pin the patch to the turning of the hole, exactly along the crease, matching the raw edges. *Figure 43.*

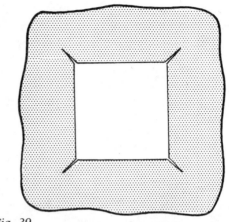

Fig. 39

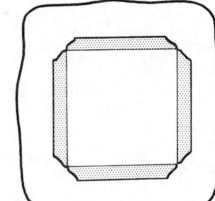

Fig. 40

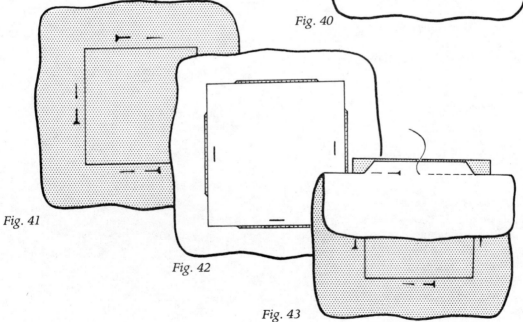

Fig. 41

Fig. 42

Fig. 43

6. Now backstitch this seam along the crease, taking the stitching right into the corner. Turn, re-fold and re-pin, and continue along the remaining three sides of the patch.

7. Mitre the corners of the patch. Press with steam, turning the edges of the patch inwards. Finish them separately with overcasting. *Figure 44.*

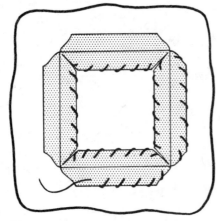

Fig. 44

8. If the patch is in a conspicuous position on a good garment, it would be worth the trouble of rantering its seams, as shown on page 41. This process, used by professional repairers, helps to blur the straight lines of the seams and render them less visible.

9. Press, and brush up any nap on the right side.

The Fine-Drawn Patch
This patch is a classic form of invisible mending or re-weaving. It is a nice point whether it should be classed as a patch or a darn, as the edges of the patch are fringed to fit the hole, and then darned in.

French re-weaving produces the most perfect of all repairs. But the finer points of its techniques are jealously-guarded trade secrets and take years of specialized training to acquire, which explains its very high cost. It is not work that can be undertaken by amateurs.

However, the Fine-Drawn Patch, one of the simplest forms of re-weaving, is a practical possibility if you are dealing with a fabric – such as linen or a loosely woven wool – where the threads are both individually visible and easily separable. Then, it is an extremely valuable technique. But many fabrics, particularly those made of synthetic fibres, are too finely-woven for any but professional workers to tackle.

A strong magnifying glass should be used, as absolute precision is needed if the repair is to be invisible, and the only real difficulty lies in seeing the work clearly. The much-enlarged patch on linen, in the photographs on these pages, was worked through an eye-surgeon's *loupe* with a focus of 7cm (3in); even with this aid, it was taxing to the sight. Yet professional repairers are able to work at astonishing speed without any special aids.

1 Fine-Drawn Patch – wrong side

Bearing this warning in mind, the un-daunted should proceed as follows:

1. Snip the hole into a square or rectangle, using fine, sharp embroidery scissors. Cut out the broken and damaged threads only – *not one more. Figure 45.*

2. Cut the patch, which must be of the same fabric, at least 5cm (2in) larger each way than the hole. Fringe two adjacent sides of the patch to a depth of 1cm ($\frac{3}{8}$in). Now, with the wrong sides of garment and patch uppermost, and matching the direction of the warp threads, fit the fringed corner of the patch into a corner of the hole – A to A etc. If the pair of threads cut away at the corner of the hole were crossed warp-over-weft, then the pair of threads nearest the corner of the patch must be the same. Ravel another thread from the patch if necessary to make a true match. For clarity, the threads that are to be woven in are shown shaded. *Figure 46.*

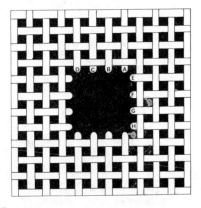

Fig. 45

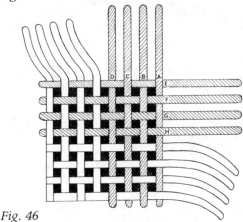

Fig. 46

2 Fine-Drawn Patch – right side

3. Pin the patch in its exact place over the hole: if you have left a good margin along the unfringed edges, pins should not impede your work – but if in doubt tack instead of pinning.

4. Thread a fine needle with a silk or slippery nylon thread, making a loop by threading both cut ends through the eye.

5. At A, pick up with the point of the needle the first three (alternate) threads under which the first of the cut threads passes. Pull through, leaving a small loop. *Figure 47.* Into this loop, (using the needle point or a fine crochet hook), slip the first thread of the patch; tighten the loop and draw it through the fabric, leaving the thread end loose on

the surface. Repeat with B, C and D in turn, along that side of the patch.

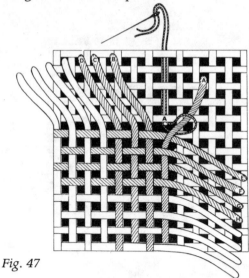

Fig. 47

It is important not to miss the *first* thread along the side of the hole. This must be picked up cleanly; if the needle splits it, or does not take it up, it will show as a 'floater' on the right side. To prevent distortion, hold the patch firmly between finger and thumb as you draw each thread through.

6. Now weave in the threads E, F, G and H, in that order, from the other fringed side of the patch. *Figure 48.*

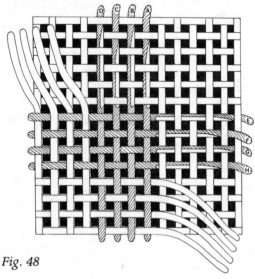

Fig. 48

36

7. When these two adjacent sides are completed, fringe the remaining sides to the exact number of threads needed. That is, leave on the patch only the other ends of the threads already woven in.

8. Weave these into the last two sides of the hole.

9. Pull up all the thread ends gently. Snip them off closely.

10. Press with steam, right side down on an unpadded board.

The repair should be totally invisible. In the right-side photograph on page 35, the patch is exactly in the centre.

The Re-Woven Patch

This is somewhat similar to the previous patch, but is the form of re-weaving more often used by professional repairers on suit-weight fabrics. It is almost equally trying to the eyes. Ideally, it should be worked with a fine latch-needle, or 'knit-picker'. *Figure 49* shows the actual size of the needle mounted in a pin-vice; it is a miniature version of the latch-hook used for knotting rugs. Failing a latch-needle, a loop of thread can be used, as for the Fine-Drawn Patch above.

Fig. 49

1. Cut the patch 2.5cm (1in) larger each way than the area to be patched. Do not cut away any of the damaged fabric round the hole.

2. Fringe the top and left-hand sides of the patch to a depth of 1cm ($\frac{3}{8}$in).

3. Pin or tack the patch in place on the right side of the hole, exactly matching the grain and any weave pattern.

Re-woven patches, worked and rantered on two sides:

3 Twilled worsted, threads hooked in pairs

4 Twilled worsted, threads hooked in 4's

5 Herringbone worsted, threads hooked in 3's

6 Hopsack worsted, threads hooked in 4's

4. Support the work on a small, firmly stuffed pad. Beginning at the top right-hand corner, insert the latch-needle 5mm ($\frac{1}{4}$in) above the patch. Bring it up at the point that will become the corner of the *patch*, about 1cm ($\frac{3}{8}$in) from its right-hand (unfringed) edge.

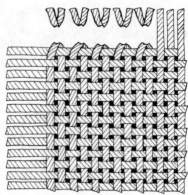

Fig. 51

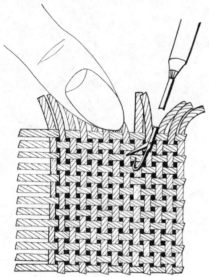

Fig. 50

5. Hook through a pair of warp threads – one of which will have passed over and the other under the top weft thread of the patch. (In the first photograph on page 37, the light-coloured threads at the right are lying in pairs, as also are the dark ones between them. They have been taken up as pairs along the top of the patch.)

As you pull the hook through, the thread ends will be brought back up to the right side, 5mm ($\frac{1}{4}$in) away from the top of the patch. With your left thumb, hold out of the way any threads you have not yet hooked in.

If the weave is not a plain one, a group of threads (not just a pair) should be taken up; in a twill, for instance, there may be 3, 4 or even 5 threads to a group, as in the other three photographs.

6. Continue along this side of the patch, taking similar pairs or groups of threads, until you reach the left-hand corner. *Figure 51*.

7. Now hook through the weft threads along the left side of the patch.

8. Fringe out the lower and right-hand edges, and work them in the same way.

9. Now that the patch is in place, it should be *rantered*. This is the term used in the trade for various methods of finishing the seams of a patch. It is always worked from the right side. In this case, its purpose is to flatten the patch edges and to secure the threads on the wrong side.

If you use a fine, matt-finished, matching thread in a fine needle, the rantering should be invisible. The best, if you can get it, is the polyester thread used for industrial overlocking. The patches photographed on page 37 have been rantered along the top and down one side; the other two sides are still unattached.

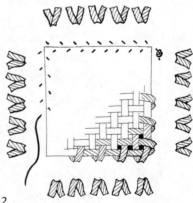

Fig. 52

Begin with a knot on the right side, which is cut off after the rantering is finished. Work in herringbone fashion, but from right to left. Bring up the needle above the patch and take a tiny diagonal stitch. The next stitch comes up on the patch itself, catching in the fabric behind. The wrong side will show diagonal stitches across the edge of the patch. Repeat these stitches alternately all round the patch. *Figure 52.*

10. Using the latch-needle or a plain needle, winkle the thread ends back to the wrong side. Apart from cutting away any loose threads round the hole itself, no finishing is needed on the wrong side.

11. Press with steam under a woollen cloth. The softer the fabric, the less this patch will show – on a blend containing polyester, for instance, it may be more visible than in these photographs of worsted and woollen suitings, which in any case have the advantage of checks as camouflage.

Patching by machine

The Tailor's Patch

Unless you are prepared to tackle the re-weaving method above, the Tailor's Patch is the best for repairs on skirts, pants, coats or men's suits. It is both stronger and more nearly invisible than the hand-set version shown on page 33. It is just as suitable for covering a three-cornered tear as a hole.

Patches larger than about 3cm (1¼in) are fairly easy to manipulate, but smaller ones are more difficult and, unless you have already worked one successfully, it is suggested that in this particular case you should choose the hand process.

1. Cut the hole into a square or oblong shape exactly along the thread of the fabric. Clip 5mm (¼in) diagonally into each corner. *Figure 53.*

2. Turn the edges of the hole back on the wrong side, and press. The creases must lie exactly along the thread of the fabric. *Figure 54.*

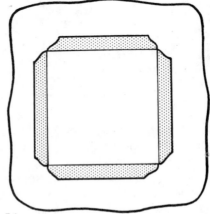

Fig. 54

3. Place the patching fabric under the prepared hole, right sides upwards, matching both the direction of the threads and any woven pattern of checks or stripes. Pin accurately in place. *Figure 55.*

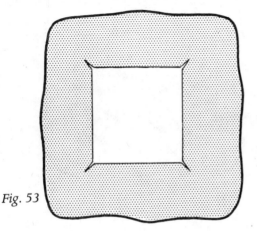

Fig. 53

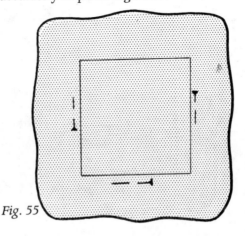

Fig. 55

4. Turn to the wrong side, and trim the patch to the same size as the hole plus its turnings, so that the edges of the patch coincide with the folded-back turnings of the hole. *Figure 56.* Leave the lower edge and sides of the patch pinned to the garment.

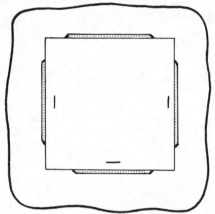

Fig. 56

5. Along the upper edge of the hole, pin together the turning and the patch. Fold back the upper part of the garment and, working with the turnings of the hole uppermost, machine along this first side. *Figure 57.* Begin one stitch only away from the corner, using a longish stitch, and work exactly along the crease – that is, along the straight grain of both garment and patch. When this seam has been worked, run off the machine stitching into the corner of the patch. Do not try to turn the corners in one continuous seam.

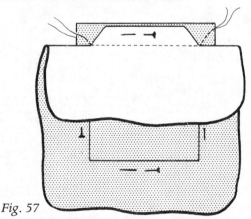

Fig. 57

40

6. Re-fold the garment, to work the next side of the patch. You should work clockwise round the hole, beginning at the corner where the previous stitching ended.

7. When all four sides have been completed, mitre the corners of the patch by cutting straight across them. *Figure 58.*

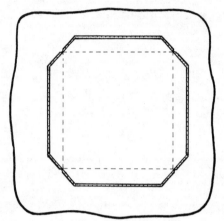

Fig. 58

8. Turn the edges of the patch inwards. Press with steam to make them lie flat against the wrong side of the patch. In commercial repairing, it is not usual to finish the edges; however, to prevent ravelling, they may if you wish be overcast separately. *Figure 59.*

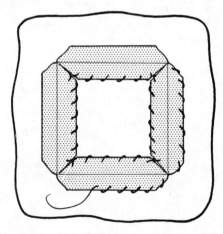

Fig. 59

9. On the right side, the patch should now be rantered, to make the seams less conspicuous. This is a different form of rantering from the one described in the last section. Its purpose is not to secure the patch but to mask the straight line of the machining.

Use a fine needle and a fine, matt-surfaced thread – a polyester thread is ideal. Do not take a thread from the fabric itself, as that would not be strong enough. If you cannot get an exact match, choose one shade darker or duller; but as a professional repairer is able to ranter in white thread on black fabric without any stitch showing, a true match is not as essential here as in some other repairs.

Begin with a knot on the right side, 3mm ($\frac{1}{8}$in) away from one corner. (This knot is cut off after the rantering is completed.) Bring the needle up precisely at the corner and take a stitch, picking up one thread only, at each side of the seam in turn. *Figure 60*. This is easiest if the work is folded along the seam, and the fold held pinched between thumb and first finger. The stitches should be taken as closely as possible to the seam, and close together; on loosely-woven fabrics, take one stitch to every alternate thread. Pull up rather tightly. Continue round all four sides of the patch.

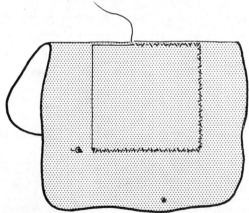

Fig. 60

By blurring the straight line of the seam, rantering makes it much less visible. The photograph on this page shows a patch with the upper and right-hand sides rantered. The lower and left-hand sides have not yet been worked, and the seamlines throw distinct shadows.

10. Finish by pressing with steam and brushing up the nap.

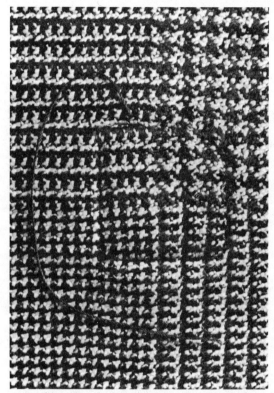

7 *Tailor's Patch, rantered on two sides only*

The Machine-Felled Patch
This machine version of the patch described on page 29 makes a repair that is stronger and quicker, and no less neat. But because there are two seams round the patch, it is necessarily one of the more visible repairs and should be used only where that does not matter.

1. Cut the patch allowing for 1cm ($\frac{3}{8}$in) turnings. Press them to the right side. *Figure 61*.

2. With garment and patch wrong sides up, centre the patch over the hole and tack it in place.

41

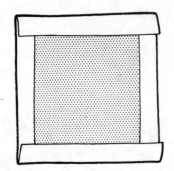

Fig. 61

3. Machine close to the edges, pivoting on the needle at each corner. *Figure 62.*

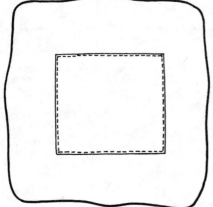

Fig. 62

4. Turn to the right side. Trim the worn fabric from round the hole to leave 1.5cm ($\frac{5}{8}$in) seam turnings inside the stitching. Clip 5mm ($\frac{1}{4}$in) into each corner. *Figure 63.*

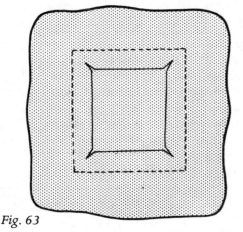

Fig. 63

5. Tuck in the turnings. Machine the four sides close to the folds. *Figure 64.*

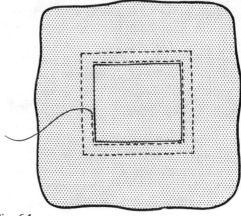

Fig. 64

The Single-Seam Patch
This patch is worked with the 3-step zig-zag stitch, set at a short length and at maximum width. It is useful for mending light-weight fabrics.

Cut the patch with turnings no wider than 5mm ($\frac{1}{4}$in) pressed to the wrong side. Tack it right side up to the right side of the fabric. Machine all round, letting the edge of the stitching fall a hairsbreadth outside the folded edges of the patch. Be sure that the corners are caught down as shown in *Figure 65*. At the back, trim off the fabric close to the stitching.

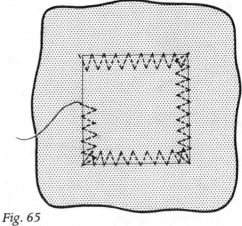

Fig. 65

The advantage of this patch is that the machining tends to flatten its edges, so blending them better into the surrounding fabric.

The Butted Patch

A variation of the last patch, this one is useful for very thick fabrics, such as coatings, where any seam-turnings would add unsightly bulk. Especially on a textured or napped fabric, it can be almost invisible. It is quite strong enough for all but those parts of a garment subjected to heavy wear.

1. Cut the hole to a clean shape, preferably without corners.
2. With right sides up, pin the patching fabric over the hole, matching the straight grain and any pattern.
3. Turn over to the wrong side. With a tailor's chalk pencil, trace through the hole the exact shape of the patch. *Figure 66*. Cut it out.

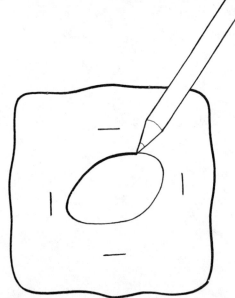

Fig. 66

4. Cut a piece of tarlatan, lining fabric or organdie, larger than the patch, as backing. Tack the patch to it, right side up. *Figure 67*.
5. Fit the hole over the reinforced patch, matching the edges precisely, and tack.

Fig. 67

6. With the 3-step zig-zag stitch set at a short length and at maximum width, machine all round the patch, letting the stitching extend equally on each side of the seam. *Figure 68*.

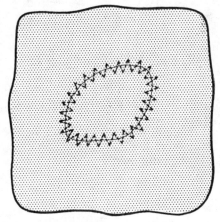

Fig. 68

7. On the wrong side, trim off the backing close to the outer edge of the stitching. Brush up the nap on the right side, and press with steam under a woollen cloth.

The Reinforcing Patch

A patch placed on the wrong side is a suitable reinforcement for an area of heavy wear, before the thin place has actually rubbed into a hole. This is a most useful repair for children's clothing and is very simple to work.

1. The patch has no turnings, so it may be cut to any shape, and finished by zig-zag stitching. It should be large enough to allow a wide surround to the thin place.

43

2. Herringbone the patch to the wrong side. *Figure 69.*

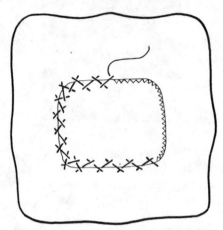

Fig. 69

3. On the right side, machine-darn the thin place to the patch.

In the repaired trouser seat photographed on page 104, the left-hand half of the patch was worked in this way.

44

REPAIRING KNITTED FABRICS

Repairing knitted fabrics

The majority of fabrics now used for clothing are knitted. Hosiery and sweaters have of course always been so, along with much underwear and nightwear. But now knitted fabrics are used for most shirts, for many women's dresses, jackets and skirts, for trousers and even for men's suits. Children's and sports clothes are increasingly made from knitted fabrics, because of their comfort, lightness and elasticity.

The very diversity of these fabrics is such that no general rules can be made for their repair. The degree of stretch, the thickness, density of construction and surface texture are almost infinitely varied. The three main classes of knitted fabric have totally different characteristics which follow from their method of construction. Here, therefore, the rules for mending are given separately for each class of fabric.

Single weft knitting

This class includes all hand-knitting and those fabrics that look like hand-knitting, where a plain stitch on the right side shows as a purl on the reverse. The fabric is constructed with a single thread, which is worked along rows of loops and which itself forms the next row. Because of their construction, these knits are stretchable in every direction, though more so across the rows than down the wale of the knit. The design of garments made from them takes into account this ability to stretch; therefore any repair must be as fully stretchable as the garment itself.

Threads used for mending should match as nearly as possible the yarn from which the garment was made. Keep oddments of wool for mending any garments you have knitted. Failing the identical yarn, choose one of the right colour and as nearly as possible of similar texture – matt or glossy, smooth or crimped. It may be slightly thinner than the thread of the garment; in fact a thinner thread may be useful for reinforcing. For instance, a matching four-ply yarn could be split to give a two-ply mending thread. While losing something in strength, it will make a smoother, less bulky repair.

The Stocking Darn
This name identifies the type of darn, not the garment. It can be used on any kind of single-knit fabric.

8 *Stocking Darn*

Everyone knows how to darn after a fashion – one has, after all, to darn so often. But the strictly correct method is given here in some detail because, even if it is not followed precisely, thread by thread and loop by loop, it gives a far better finish and longer wear –

and takes little more time – than the unin-structed cobble. It is not suggested that, faced with a pile of disintegrating socks, you should work with such meticulous accuracy; but on the other hand a perfectly worked thin-place darn at the elbow of a Cashmere sweater will make a totally invisible reinforcement.

Use a darning needle. It has a big enough eye to allow a thick thread to run smoothly, and it is long enough to work the whole length of the darn before pulling through the thread. This gives better control and saves time.

1. Cut the hole to an even shape, snipping the sides cleanly up the wale of the knit, the same number of rows on each side, and leaving a single clear row of loops along the top and bottom edges. In *Figure 70*, the top row has two loops and two halves, while the bottom row has three complete loops. (Attempt such cutting only where you can see the loops; if the knitting is at all felted, as in the toe of a sock, it is better not to cut the hole to shape but simply to darn in the loose edges.)

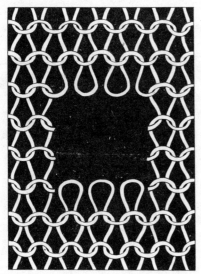

Fig. 70

2. Darns are always worked from the wrong side. Most people find it best to hold the work spread between the bent first and second fingers of the left hand. The warp or vertical strands are laid first; hold your hand with the thumb towards you, and point the needle alternately towards and away from you. The weft or crosswise set of threads can then be laid in the same way, simply by giving a quarter-turn to your hand, so that the palm is towards you. There is then no need to rearrange the work on your fingers. Alternatively, a wooden or plastic darning mushroom may be preferred. Be careful not to over-stretch the hole as you work; if you do, the finished darn will stand up like a blister.

3. The stitches of knitting are formed by the *upward-pointing* purl loops in the web. The first darning strand takes up every alternate one. The return journey is made *between* the stitches, taking up every alternate *downward-pointing* loop. *Figure 71*.

Purl loop at top of stitch

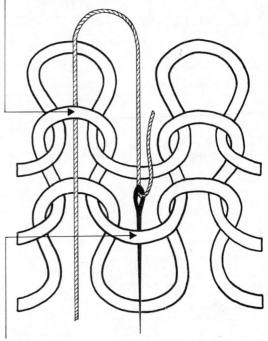

Purl loop between stitches

Fig. 71

4. Begin darning at the lower left-hand corner, two or three stitches to the left of the hole and two or three rows down, depending

on the texture of the knit. If there is any thin part around the hole, the darn must extend in all directions into sound fabric.

Starting at A, *Figure 72*, pick up cleanly each alternate upward-facing loop. Do not dig indiscriminately into the knitted web; if the purl loop *only* is picked up, the darn will be invisible in the area surrounding the hole. Work the first strand up to two or three rows above the hole, picking up the loops in succession on the needle. Do not draw the thread through until you reach the top.

5. Lay the return strand by taking up the next higher purl loop on the right, *between* the knit stitches: it will be a downward-pointing one. Continue downwards, leaving a small loop of darning thread where you have turned. The purpose of this loop is to allow for shrinkage of the new thread; but more importantly to allow movement in the finished darn, so that the ends of the rows do not pull and distort the knitting.

6. The shape of the darn should be octagonal, as shown. The first strand is the shortest. A stitch is added at the top and bottom of each subsequent strand until the maximum depth of the darn is reached, at the left-hand side of the hole. This depth is maintained until the right-hand side is reached, when the strands are again shortened.

7. Be sure to pick up every loop along the upper and lower edges of the hole. This will stop these loops from curling up ostentatiously on the right side of the darn, and will also prevent ladders.

8. When all the vertical strands are worked, cut off the thread at B.

9. Now work the weft strands. These are spaced level with, and between, each purl row. Weave the needle through the previously-laid warp strands, picking them up alternately. On the return journey, take up the strands you passed over before. *Do not pick up any loops of the knitted web; this is*

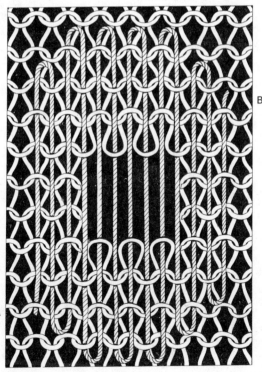

Fig. 72

Fig. 73

important if the darn is to be inconspicuous. Begin at A, *Figure 73*, and finish at B. Notice that these weft threads do not cover the whole area of the darn. They form a rectangle, extending only as far as the shortest of the warp strands.

10. The finished darn should show clean, close weaving on the right side of the hole, and no stitches whatever in the knitted web around it. See the photograph on page 47.

The Thin-Place Stocking Darn
This is worked in exactly the same way as the previous darn, except that the vertical strands only are laid. Unless the thin place is literally threadbare, no transverse strands should be needed.

As before, only the alternate purl loops are picked up, so that no stitch penetrates to the right side, and the darn is totally invisible.

Knitting up a Ladder
This operation is very simple if you use a crochet hook of the right size – as fine a one as will pick up a thread without splitting it. Work from the right or plain side of the knitting, as shown in *Figure 74*.

Slip the hook into the loop at the bottom of the ladder. Pass it *under* the thread above, and pull through. This is important: if you pass the hook *over* the thread, it will twist the loops in the repaired ladder. Continue in this way to the top of the ladder and secure the last loop with needle and thread.

If several stitches have laddered, pass a thread through their loops so that they do not run any further while you are working.

In commercial repair work, ladders are knitted up with a latch-needle like the one shown on page 36. It was used even for ladders in fine stockings and tights; but this is no longer done because it is now cheaper to replace hosiery than to repair it.

Machining up a Ladder
The ladder may be too fine to be knitted up, or the condition of the garment may not warrant the amount of work. In that case, a quick repair can be made with the machine zig-zag stitch, set wide enough to span the ladder. This will pull together the extra width caused by the dropped stitch, and so make the ladder less noticeable. *Figure 75.*

Fig. 74

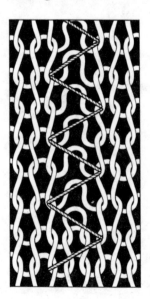

Fig. 75

Grafting

If a thread has been pulled out of the knitted web, and broken, you will be faced with two rows of loops pointing towards each other. Probably you will also find a line of tightly-pulled stitches at each end of the damage. These must first be loosened back to their original tension, with the point of a needle, even if it means extending the length of the graft.

Begin two or three stitches to the right of the damage, with matching yarn in a blunt (tapestry) needle. Work from the right side, as shown in *Figure 76*.

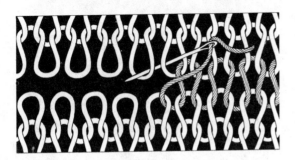

Fig. 76

Grafting simply consists of two repeated steps. First, pass the needle *down* into one loop and *up* out of the next loop to the left. Then, in the other row, move back half a loop and again work down and up through two adjacent loops.

If the knit pattern is not a plain stocking stitch – if, for instance, it is a rib – then the loops of any purl stitches must be picked up from *underneath*, so that a purl loop is formed on the right side.

Working back a Snag

A thread snagged but not actually broken should be worked back along, the row, as above. Any residual loop should be threaded into a large-eyed needle – poked up eye-first from the reverse of the fabric – and drawn through to the wrong side.

The Swiss Darn

While Stocking Darning imitates the warp and weft of woven fabric, the Swiss Darn imitates the web of knitting. It does not by itself cover a hole, but it is most useful for the totally invisible reinforcement of thin areas.

There are two variants of Swiss Darning. The horizontal type is stronger, as it forms a complete new web worked over and into the old one.

1. Use a blunt-pointed tapestry needle to avoid splitting stitches. Begin at the lower right-hand corner of the thin place and darn towards the left in the exact pattern of the web, and at the same tension, following the thread along a row of stitches. This is shown as the lowest shaded row in *Figure 77*.

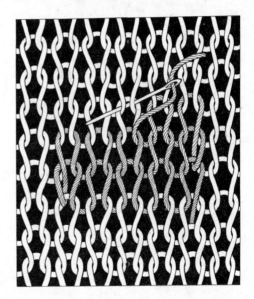

Fig. 77

2. At the end of the row, take the needle down through a loop and bring it up into the next loop above.
3. Turn the darn upside-down and work the next row, again moving from right to left. Repeat these rows as far as necessary, being sure to cover the whole thin area. Cut off the thread on the wrong side, and press lightly under a damp cloth.

The other type of Swiss Darning is worked vertically up and down the wale of the knit, instead of along a row. As the successive strands do not link into each other, this repair is not so strong as the previous one. It also takes longer to work. It is, however, included for the sake of completeness.

1. Bring the needle up in the centre of a loop at the lower right-hand corner, as in *Figure 78*. Move up a row and pick up the right-hand thread of the next loop. Repeat as far upwards as necessary.

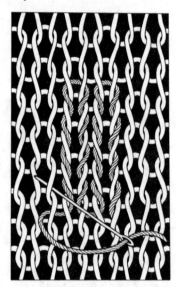

Fig. 78

2. To begin the second line of darning, take the needle under *both* the threads of a loop; then (without turning the work) proceed down the second side of the same stitches, again taking up a single thread at each level.

The diagram shows more of the knitted web than will actually be seen. In finished appearance, there is in fact no difference between the two types of Swiss Darning.

The Stocking Web Darn

This type of darn, worked accurately and at the right tension, will make a perfectly invisible repair over a hole. The time and patience needed for its execution would be well rewarded if an expensive sweater were thereby restored to the front of your wardrobe. This darn, incidentally, is one of those precise but repetitive activities that can prove distinctly soothing and therapeutic – 'a knitter drowsed, whose fingers play in skilled unmindfulness'.

1. First trim the hole into a square or oblong, leaving a clear row of loops at the top and bottom. At the corners, unravel a couple of stitches, so that each side of the hole becomes a turning which can be folded back, like the shutters of a window, along the line of a stitch. *Figure 79*.

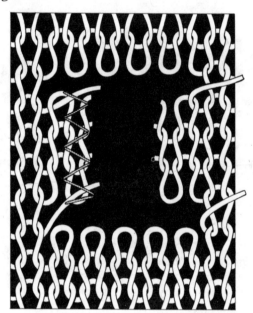

Fig. 79

2. Secure the edge of each turning with widely-spaced machine zig-zag stitching or with hand overcasting. Fold the turnings to the wrong side and tack them temporarily out of the way. You will be left with a clean rectangular hole, in this case with four whole loops and two halves across the top, and five whole loops across the bottom.

3. The darn is constructed on foundation threads stretched over the hole. Use ordinary sewing thread and begin with a large knot on the wrong side. Bring the thread up through

the right-hand loop of the bottom row. *Figure 80*. Move to the top row of loops; insert the needle into the right-hand half-loop and bring it up through the next loop to the left. Move to the bottom row again, into the first loop and up through the next to the left. Continue in this way to the last loop on the left, and secure the thread temporarily at the back of the work. The wrong side of the darn at this stage is shown in the photograph on page 54.

It is all too easy to lay these foundation threads too tightly; they must be loose enough to allow a little stretch in the fabric round the hole.

4. The darn is worked from the right side, with exactly-matching yarn. Begin two stitches to the right of the bottom row of loops. *Figure 81*. Work these two stitches in horizontal Swiss Darning, as shown on page 51. Now, bringing the needle up in the first free loop, pass it behind the pair of foundation threads and back into the same loop again. Bring it up in the next loop and continue in this way to the last of the free loops. End the row with two stitches of Swiss Darning into the fabric. It is immaterial whether or not the turning at the back of the work is caught into the darn.

5. Turn the darn upside-down and work across the hole in the same way, into the loops you made on the first journey. Continue until the number of rows worked is one fewer than the rows up the side of the hole. (In this case, you will have worked four rows.) The fifth and last row is formed by grafting into the loops left along the top of the hole. Finish with two Swiss Darning stitches into the top left-hand corner.

6. At the back of the work, cut off the knot of the foundation thread. If the rest of the thread does not show on the right side, there is no need to remove it, but each vertical bar should be snipped at some point so that the darn becomes fully elastic.

7. If the side turnings have not been caught into the Swiss Darning, they may either be trimmed off or left in place, pressed flat behind the darn. Which you choose should depend on the density of the web and the bulkiness of the turnings themselves. The darn is quite safely anchored without them.

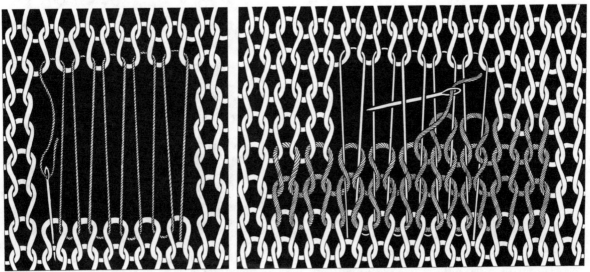

Fig. 80   Fig. 81

9 *Foundation threads for Stocking Web Darn*

The Knitted Patch

This method is better than the Stocking Web Darn for all but the smallest holes. Over a large area, it gives a more even texture and takes considerably less time to work. Its only disadvantage is that the side edges of the patch may show up a little more clearly than if they were Swiss-darned.

Use the wool and the size of needle with which the garment was originally made.

1. First, cut the hole into a square or oblong, taking out all the thin part round the hole. Leave a clear row of loops at the top and bottom. At the corners, unravel stitches as above, to form side turnings. Overlock their edges and tack them down on the wrong side. They will remain in place behind the finished patch. *Figure 82.*

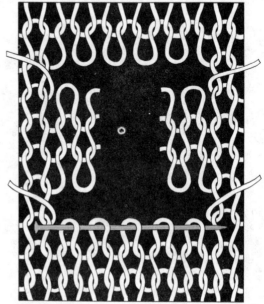

Fig. 82

2. Pick up on a knitting needle all the stitches along the bottom of the hole. Begin knitting (in the same pattern as the rest of the garment) at the lower right-hand corner, leaving a long free end of yarn to be used later for darning in the side of the patch.

3. Knit up the appropriate number of rows, as in *Figure 83*. Now cut the yarn, leaving a long end.

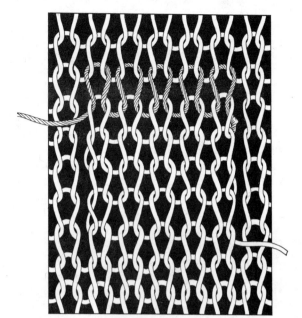

Fig. 84

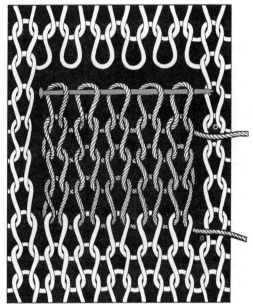

Fig. 83

4. Thread this end into a tapestry needle, and graft the stitches from the knitting needle to the loops across the top of the hole, as shown in *Figure 84*. Finish at the top left-hand corner, ready to work down the left side of the patch.

5. Weave the yarn as shown in *Figure 85*, beginning at the arrow. Work first to the left, into the garment, then down to bridge the gap, and then to the right into the last stitch of the patch. (This is really a very narrow version of Swiss Darning.) Continue downwards until the side of the patch is completed. Lead the yarn away through two loops on the wrong side, and cut off.

6. Now work the right-hand side of the patch in the same way, using the long end of yarn you left at the beginning.

Fig. 85

7. Press very lightly under a damp woollen cloth. The patch should blend invisibly at top and bottom, with only the slightest line showing down each side.

8. If the patch can be planned to extend into a seam down one side, this will give a neater and simpler finish.

55

The Couched Darn

Many knitted fabrics are of too close a texture for the foregoing repairs to be practicable, but they may be darned instead with a couched woollen thread. This can give a good matching texture, but there will be little stretch in the darn.

The Couched Darn can be worked only if your machine has a darning foot with a slot in its toe to guide in the wool. A bare needle, unsupported by the foot, will not produce a satisfactory result.

1. Fit the darning foot and adjust the machine according to the instructions in the machine booklet. Slot in the couching thread.
2. Drop the feed-dog teeth.
3. Set the zig-zag stitch wide enough to span the couching thread. The stitch-length is immaterial; the faster you move the work, the more widely-spaced the stitches will be.
4. Work parallel rows, close together, turning the work at the end of each row. It should not be necessary to lay a second set of strandings across the first. *Figure 86.*

It is, however, far from inconspicuous so it is better used for underwear than for outer garments.

1. Cut the patch, preferably with rounded corners, and with no turnings. Tack it to the *right* side of the hole.
2. Set the 3-step zig-zag stitch at a short length and at medium width. You should test the stitch length to be sure that it does not over-stretch the fabric. Stitch round the edge of the patch: if you work as suggested from the right side, you can be sure that the edge of the patch does not become distorted.
3. Turn over to the wrong side. Work a second row of stitching 1cm ($\frac{3}{8}$in) inside the first row, and trim off the damaged part close to the stitching. *Figure 87.*

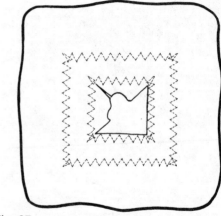

Fig. 87

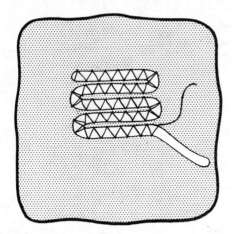

Fig. 86

The Stretchable Machined Patch

On such materials as stockinette, this method gives a serviceable, stretchable patch – the machined version of the Herringboned Patch.

Fig. 88

In a variation of this patch, a single seam can be used, similar to the one shown on page 42 but without turnings. It is worked from the right side, as above, but with the widest setting of the 3-step zig-zag. The worn part on the wrong side may be left in place, to give strength to the patch. *Figure 88*.

Double weft knitting
Double knitting, or double jersey, has a good claim to be the most awkward of all fabrics to mend satisfactorily. You can quite easily throw a stretchable seam round a patch, but it is likely to show up like a beacon. Before deciding on any patch or darn, consider one of the camouflage methods shown on page 73.

Double knitting is easy to identify because both sides have the appearance of stocking stitch. The structure is like a sandwich, with the purl loops turned inwards between the layers. To hold the layers together, an intermittent row of stitches picks up a loop alternately from each side. In *Figure 89*, the shaded threads show the face of the fabric and the hatched threads the reverse; the white thread passes between the two.

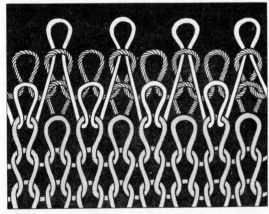

Fig. 89

Although it is knitted with threads laid weftwise, it has much more dimensional stability than single knitting. It is firm, resilient and recovers well from creasing.

It stretches less up-and-down than across the rows, so skirts and pants resist 'seating' very well.

Any fibre can be double-knit, but the heavier suit-weights are usually of wool, acrylic (such as Acrilan or Courtelle) or crimped polyester (such as Crimplene). Thinner fabrics made from cotton or rayon (or both) are widely used for T-shirts, underpants etc. The lightest quality, a fine, supple jersey which drapes and gathers beautifully, is made of silk or polyester. As this is most often used for blouses or evening wear, its repair presents the worst problem of all. The threads of this fine jersey are easily split or broken by an ordinary machine-needle, and are then liable to run. To avoid this, use a ball-point machine-needle which has a rounded tip designed to slide between the threads.

Probably the best patch (depending on the fabric) would be the Tailor's Patch on page 39, with its sides worked in a very narrow zig-zag stitch to allow for some stretch, or in the jersey stretch-stitch found on automatic machines. Rantering, as shown under the Tailor's Patch, will make a deal of difference to its visibility on a springy fabric. For underwear, use a top-stitched patch, worked with the 3-step zig-zag stitch, as shown in the photograph on page 115.

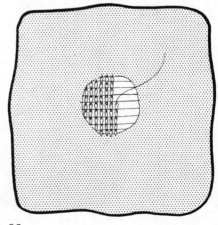

Fig. 90

For a small hole, a darn would be better than a patch. On heavier-weight jersey, a Stocking Darn (page 47) should serve best, as it keeps the area of repair as small as possible. But for a small hole on fine jersey, it may be possible to imitate the Stocking Web Darn (page 52) by laying only *weftwise* foundation threads, and working over them, on the right side, rows of very fine chain-stitch. *Figure 90.*

Warp knitting

The structure of this fabric is quite different from weft knitting, and fabrics made in this way have quite dissimilar properties. It is knitted from as many warp threads as there are stitches across the fabric; the loops appear to form vertical lines of stitches, but in fact the threads are taken diagonally, alternately to right and left, to lock into nearby stitches. *Figure 91* shows the simplest form of warp knitting, where each thread moves only one stitch sideways. It is easier to recognize warp knitting from the reverse of the fabric, where the transverse threads form horizontal ridges.

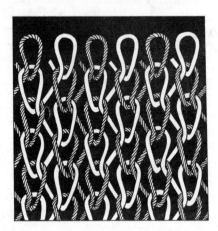

Fig. 91

Warp knitting is dense, resists laddering and has very little stretch in either direction. A variation of warp knitting, called Raschel, can reproduce the effect of lace.

Warp-knit fabrics can be made from any fibre, but perhaps the most extensive use is for nylon shirtings. Very sheer materials for underwear and evening wear are also usually warp-knit from nylon. Apart from these transparent fabrics, warp-knits should be repaired as if they were woven. Any patch or darn suitable for woven fabric of a similar weight will also be suitable for a warp-knit. In contrast to repairs on double knitting, these blend reasonably well.

The Top-Stitched Seam

Particularly suitable for repairs on warp-knit lingerie, the top-stitched seam shown in the photograph on page 115 will also make a neat right-side patch. Set a medium zig-zag or a short 3-step zig-zag stitch, and work over the narrowly-folded edges of the patch.

The Overlocked Seam

On sheer materials, any repair will show through. Camouflage, by seaming out the damaged part, is the best solution; usually sheer fabrics are made up into generously full styles, so there should be little difficulty.

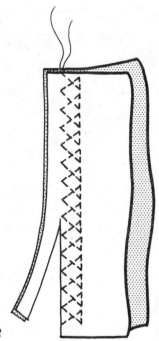

Fig. 92

As the edges will show through the fabric, any seam must be very narrowly finished. The best seam is one where the seam itself and the overlocking are worked as one process. If the stitch shown in *Figure 92* is built into your machine, it should be worked with 1cm (⅜in) seam allowances. After working the seam, trim the edges close to the stitching; this gives a better finish than trying to work exactly along the edges, which tend to curl.

The Tricot Seam
If you cannot work the above stitch, use this seam instead.
1. With right sides together, work a straight-stitched seam.
2. Press open the turnings.
3. From the right side, work a row of zig-zag or 3-step zig-zag stitching centred down the seamline, to hold the turnings flat.
4. Trim the turnings close to the stitching. *Figure 93.*

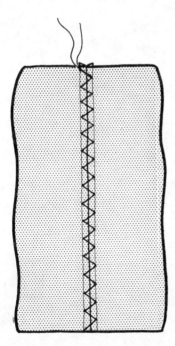

Fig. 93

REPAIRING SPECIALIZED MATERIALS

Repairing specialized materials

Leather and Suede

The mending of leather needs quite different methods from those you would use on cloth. Before attempting any repair, you should become familiar with the special problems and techniques.

Buying Leather

Small patches can usually be taken from inside pockets or facings. You will then be sure of matching the colour, texture and thickness of the leather. But often larger pieces are needed, to replace whole panels of a garment; it can be a problem to find the right leather.

Many firms offer wide ranges of leather products. These will sell in small quantities:

Amber Leather Co., 835 San Julian, Los Angeles, CA 90052

Caldwell Lace Leather Co., Auburn, KY 42206

Charles Horowitz & Sons, Inc., 25 Great Jones Street, New York, NY 10014

Needles and Threads

Use a gloving needle for hand sewing, or a leather needle in the machine. They are spear-pointed to pierce the leather more easily. Failing a leather needle, use an ordinary heavy machine needle, size 100 (U.S. size 16). Set a long machine stitch, as needle punctures close together tend to weaken the structure of leather. Buttonhole twist is suitable for both the needle and bobbin threads; or a linen or heavy polyester thread may be used – cotton is not strong enough. For top-stitching, try to match that already on the garment.

Pounding

Leather can be pressed with a dry iron, set as for wool, under brown paper instead of a pressing cloth which could leave flecks of lint on the surface. *Steam must never be used*, nor must the iron come into direct contact with the leather. But a safer alternative is pounding.

Pounding, that is tapping lightly with a smooth-faced hammer, compresses the thickness of the skin and will persuade seam turnings to lie quite flat. By spreading the leather laterally, pounding is also useful for bringing together two torn edges, or for making a butted patch fit perfectly.

Sticking

Adhesives are widely employed in the manufacture of leather garments, for holding seam turnings and hems, and for applying facings. Use Bostik 1 Clear Adhesive; this is the only cement available in the UK that will stand dry-cleaning without the danger of its melting out and discolouring the right side of the leather or suède. Liquid Hide Glue and Tandy Leather-craft Cement are similar products available in the USA. Fusible webbings such as Bondaweb (UK) and Polyweb (USA) are quite safe.

Panel Replacement

Damage to leather garments is most often caused by too tight a fit, which can strain armholes or seams. The first photograph on page 64 shows just such a case. A larger repair than a patch is needed; the whole panel should be replaced. Here, a new panel was inserted from the yoke seam down to the pocket, as shown in the second photograph.

1. Unpick the lining far enough to give yourself room to work.

 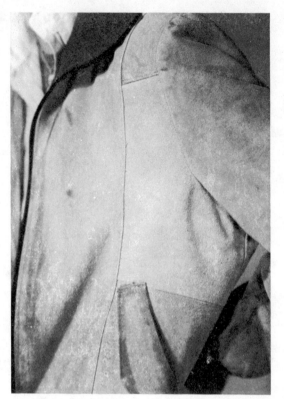

10 Suède jacket before repair

11 The same jacket, with panel replaced to pocket level

2. Unpick the affected seams – in this case, the armhole, side and side-front seams, and the yoke.

3. Use the damaged panel as a pattern for its replacement, allowing for turnings at pocket level.

4. Work the yoke and pocket-level seams first, then the side and side-front seams. Match whatever type of seam was used before; here, both topstitching and wrong-side seaming were used. If the seam turnings are to lie apart, pound them gently open and hold them down with a trace of adhesive.

5. Stitch the armhole seam.

6. Stitch the pocket back over the new panel.

7. You now have the problem of balancing up the design on the other front of the jacket. A mock seam – just a line of straight top-stitching – would simulate the new pocket-level seam. (A real seam should not be made, as

it would pull up and wrinkle that side of the jacket.)

8. Replace the lining.

Patches

A patch is less noticeable if it is butted with an adhesive backing, rather than stitched in place.

1. Cut the hole to an even, rounded shape, using sharp scissors. (Knives or razor blades are a menace on leather unless you are used to them.)

2. Place a piece of paper under the hole. Through the hole, pencil its outline on the paper. Cut out the template, turn it over and draw round its edge on to the back of the patching leather, matching the direction of any discernible grain pattern. Cut out the patch. *Figure 94.*

3. Fit the patch into the hole, wrong sides up.

64

Pound gently until they fit perfectly together.

4. Cut a piece of firm cotton or light canvas as a backing, at least 2cm ($\frac{3}{4}$in) larger all round than the patch. Coat it with adhesive and apply immediately to the patch and its surround. Leave under a weight for half an hour.

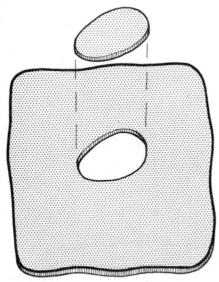

Fig. 94

Tears

A tear can be mended in just the same way, if the edges fit together cleanly after pounding.

Stitched Repairs

If the patch or tear is in a position where it will be exposed to hard wear or rubbing, it should be given an adhesive backing and then stitched. Use the 3-step zig-zag, set long and and wide. Work once only round the hole, centering the stitches over the join. Pull the thread ends through to the wrong side, knot them and secure with a trace of Bostik.

Cuts

The edges of a clean cut can be drawn together by hand, almost invisibly on leather and quite invisibly on suède.

Work with a silk or polyester thread, from the wrong side. Begin with a knot, as in *Figure*

95. Take a slanting stitch, not right through to the surface of the leather, but half-way through its thickness, to come out at one side of the cut. Repeat from the other side. Work these stitches along the cut, no closer together than 3mm ($\frac{1}{8}$in). No stitch should penetrate to the right side of the leather.

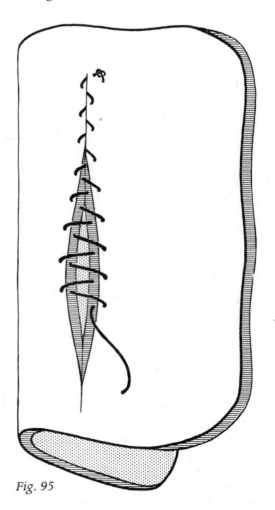

Fig. 95

Snags

A handy and simple little repair, this is sometimes needed where the surface grain has been snagged but the leather has not been torn right through. These snags can be stuck down with clear nail polish, which marries well with the nitro-cellulose finish of grain-leather. This treatment is not suitable for suède.

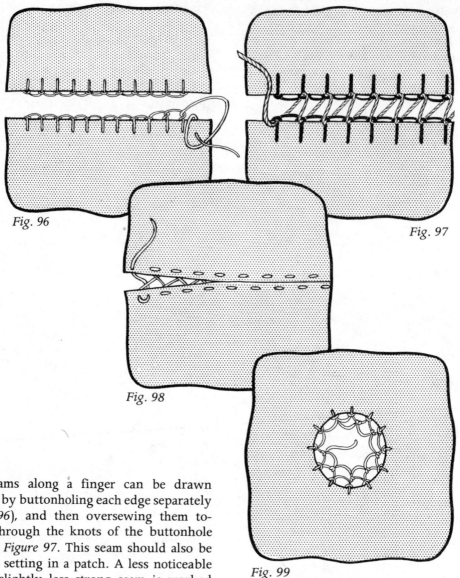

Fig. 96

Fig. 97

Fig. 98

Fig. 99

Gloves

Split seams along a finger can be drawn together by buttonholing each edge separately (*Figure 96*), and then oversewing them together through the knots of the buttonhole stitches. *Figure 97*. This seam should also be used for setting in a patch. A less noticeable though slightly less strong seam is worked with the stoting stitch, a form of herringbone shown in *Figure 98*. This is useful where a narrow overlocked side seam has split; no width is lost in turnings.

Holes should be mended by buttonhole stitches worked in diminishing circles. Each stitch is worked into the loop *between* two stitches in the previous ring. Decrease as you progress, to keep the darn flat. Finish off securely in the centre. *Figure 99*.

Pile weaves

Pile weaves include, as well as the warp and weft threads, a third or filling thread looped above the surface. In towelling, this loop is left intact: in velvet, it is sheared to leave the thread ends standing up from the fabric.

Terry Towelling

Can be very satisfactorily darned or patched with the 3-step zig-zag set at a long stitch and at maximum width. Rows of darning should be spaced fairly wide apart to avoid flattening too much the texture of the loops. A reinforcing patch, without turnings, can be applied to the right side. Again, the stitching across it should be widely spaced. The edge of the patch will be well masked by the surface texture.

Velvet

The most difficult of all fabrics to repair inconspicuously. A hand-set patch, as shown on page 33, could be used on a part of the garment that will not show much, such as under an armhole; but there is no use pretending that it will be other than an eyesore. Even professional repair firms are unwilling to undertake the patching of velvet.

The only satisfactory course would be to try one of the camouflage methods described on page 73 or to replace the whole panel (page 75).

Corduroy

A ribbed form of velvet but usually made of cotton, has a dense, short pile. It can be hand-patched, as shown on page 33, taking the vertical seams along a rib of the fabric. The seams across the ribs, however, will show up clearly as it will be found impossible to match rib to rib as if they were woven stripes. The pile itself will prevent this, forcing the ribs to alternate with each other. Again, camouflage is the best answer.

Fake Fur

The pile of these fabrics may be made to imitate almost any kind of fur from the long and silky to the short and tightly curled. Usually, the pile is nylon or acrylic; the backing fabric may be cotton or a synthetic fibre, either woven or knitted. In any case, the pile will be dense enough to hide the outline of a patch. The butted patch, applied with adhesive as to leather, will give a very good result.

Do not use scissors here, because they will sever the pile. Instead, cut the fabric from the wrong side with a razor blade, through the backing only; then pull the pile apart. When applying the patch, be sure to match the direction of the pile and to see that none of it is caught into the sides of the patch. Rather than Bostik, you may find that a fusible interfacing such as Vilene or Staflex is heavy enough; it may be ironed on with steam.

Laminated fabrics

These are constructed in three layers, like a sandwich. The face material is backed by a layer of polyurethane foam, itself backed by a thin knit. Thus, a flimsy fabric can be given body, weight and warmth.

It might be possible to work a Tailor's Patch as shown on page 39, complete with rantering. Otherwise, use a butted patch with fusible interfacing such as Vilene or Staflex; normal steam and heat will not damage the foam. This can be quite successful on a part of the garment that will not receive heavy wear.

Felt

As this is a non-woven fabric, the edges may pull out roughly if torn. It is best to cut the damaged part into an evenly-shaped hole and apply a butted patch, as above, or with the 3-step zig-zag stitch as shown on page 115. Finish by pressing, heavily, on the right side.

Vinyl

Much used for rainwear, polyvinylchloride (PVC) is a leatherlike plastic, usually supported by a thin woven or knitted backing.

The most likely damage would be a three-cornered tear. This can be almost invisibly mended with an adhesive backing. Although there are proprietary adhesive materials for rainwear, these are not usually suitable for vinyl as they need to be ironed on; but vinyl is liable to melt or go tacky under heat, so it is safer to use a cold adhesive. Cut the backing from a thin material such as poplin. Coat it with Bostik 1 Clear Adhesive and apply it to the back of the tear.

A hole in vinyl cannot be mended by sticking an overlapping patch behind it, because there is at present no adhesive that will stick vinyl to vinyl. A butted patch, using Bostik or Leathercraft Cement, would however be possible.

Sheer fabrics

Sheer woven fabrics are almost impossible to mend. The lightest of darns in the finest silk

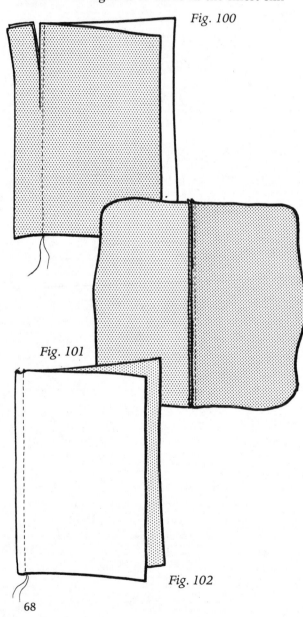

Fig. 100

Fig. 101

Fig. 102

would be clearly visible, while any patch would shine like a good deed in a naughty world. Or perhaps the other way round.

It would be best, if at all possible, to seam out the damaged part, using either the Overlocked Seam or the Tricot Seam as suggested on page 58 for knitted sheers.

An alternative would be a very fine French Seam, 3mm ($\frac{1}{8}$in) wide. On the straight grain, this is not difficult. Work the first seam with wrong sides together and trim the turnings to 2mm ($\frac{1}{16}$in). *Figure 100*. Press them to one side (*Figure 101*), then press the seam with right sides together so that the stitching falls exactly along the crease. *Figure 102*. Work the second seam 3mm ($\frac{1}{8}$in) in from the first.

Lace

It is essential to distinguish between antique hand-made laces and modern machine-made ones. They should be treated entirely differently. Hand-made lace may or may not be valuable, but it is always beautiful, rare and irreplaceable. Machine-made lace (which can indeed imitate the original very closely) is sturdy, hard-wearing and mostly machine-washable.

Hand-Made Lace

These fine laces, almost all of them over 100 years old, are now once more in fashion. So long as no strain is put on them, there is no reason why they should not again be worn as collars, edgings or shawls – which, after all, is their proper purpose. Most of them are made of very fine, highly-twisted flax threads and are a good deal stronger than their fragile appearance would suggest.

There are two kinds of hand-made lace. Needlepoint laces, worked with a single thread in a needle, are built up from many varieties of buttonhole stitch (there are actually 40 of them), often on a needle-made net ground. Their widths vary. Chantilly, a silk lace with widely spaced flower motifs on a net ground, may be wide enough for a skirt or a wedding veil. Venetian needlepoint, made from a flax thread, is stiff, heavily encrusted and usually designed in smaller pieces for collars, cuffs, lappets or borders.

Bobbin or pillow laces, on the other hand, are made by twisting and plaiting together the threads from a number of bobbins, to a pattern mapped out by pins on the lace pillow. This is really a form of weaving; it produces an essentially narrow lace, often with one edge scalloped, though it can later be put together into wider pieces. Examples are the Valenciennes lingerie or baby-lace, usually made of fine cotton. The lovely Brussels laces are basically bobbin-made but may have needle-point motifs applied to the underlying pattern.

The repair of old lace is the most highly-skilled work imaginable. Advice can be sought from museums, from the Embroiderers' Guild at Hampton Court Palace, London, or from the Embroiderers' Guild of New York City. You should never attempt a do-it-yourself repair, which might damage the lace itself, or make later restoration more difficult. However, damaged pieces can quite safely be supported on tulle; this operation can do no harm to the lace, and could make it wearable without risk.

In mending lace itself, a thread of matching weight and fibre would be used. But simply for securing the lace to the supporting tulle, either silk threads, fine 60 cotton or even polyester threads are suitable, so long as they are worked with a fine needle.

The edges of the tear or hole should be caught down over the tulle with tiny, widely-spaced hemming stitches, first to secure the edges of the damage, and then about 2cm ($\frac{3}{4}$in) away from it, behind the lace. Avoid straight lines; if possible, work along the side of a motif in the lace. *Figure 103*. Trim off the surplus tulle, taking the greatest care not to snip a thread of the lace. If the damage is along an edge, the tulle should be folded double behind the edge. An alternative method is to darn the lace lightly to the tulle backing, in one direction only.

Heavier laces can be mounted on nylon or terylene net. This support is all that will be needed, and net itself will blend with the mesh of the lace.

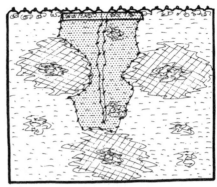

Fig. 103

Machine-Made Lace

Virtually all modern lace – certainly all that on ready-made garments – is machine-made, normally of nylon. The Leavers and Schiffli machines can imitate perfectly the bobbin and needle-made laces, and their finest products (if worked with the same threads) are almost indistinguishable from the originals.

Nylon lace is extremely hard-wearing, can be machine-washed and needs no ironing. Dress-width laces, known as allovers or flouncings, should not be washed. All can be repaired in the same way, by machine.

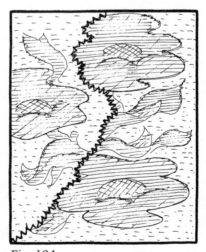

Fig. 104

Patches of lace or net, placed under the lace, should be inserted with a narrow zig-zag seam following the outline of one of the lace motifs; they should then be quite invisible. *Figure 104.* The edges of a tear can be drawn together over a net backing, and stitched with a 3-step zig-zag. Long tears can be stitched with their edges narrowly overlapped, without a backing; the edges should first be tacked together, otherwise it is difficult to keep them level and matched.

Methods of replacing the worn lace trimming on a garment are shown on page 113.

Fur

Treat all furs very gently. The skins of almost all are papery-thin and easily torn. Exceptions are such furs as Lucca and Beaver Lamb, which are sheepskins, and the flat furs such as ponyskin.

Split Seams

In the working of it, fur may have been cut into narrow strips and reassembled to elongate the pelt; or larger areas may have been built up from smaller pieces. In consequence, the skin side of a fur garment will usually show a mass of interlocking diagonal or wavy seams. If one of these splits, the damage may not be noticed until the split has lengthened and parted the covering fur.

Although furs are made up by machine, do not attempt any repair except by hand. It is enough simply to oversew the two edges together – not too tightly – with a No. 9 or 10 needle and a fine thread drawn over a piece of beeswax. Hold the seam edges pinched between your finger and thumb, with the fur sides together, and stroke all stray hairs down between the two layers with your needle. The stitches should be taken just far enough from the edges – between 2 and 3mm $\left(\frac{1}{16} - \frac{1}{8}\text{in}\right)$ – to be safe from tearing the skin.

Torn Edges

A tear at the edge of a piece of fur should be reinforced. The edges will already be taped, and most probably there will be a jap silk staying fabric well. When you have seamed the tear, oversew a short length of narrow black tape along the edge of the piece, to take any strain.

Patches

In setting in a fur patch, not only must you match the direction in which the fur lies, but also its density and character. Cut the patch with a razor blade, drawing it gently over the skin side and easing – not cutting – the fur apart. Oversew in place as for a tear.

The working of fur is a highly skilled craft, and it would be wise to get professional help rather than attempt any more extensive repairs than those described.

REPAIRING GARMENTS

Repairing garments

No two repairs need quite the same treatment; it is important to choose the most appropriate method for the case in hand. The question is not simply, 'Shall I darn or shall I patch?' There may be a better way.

The shape and cut of the garment, and the position and size of the damage should be considered carefully before you start any repair, as they should influence your choice of method.

Camouflage

This is a matter of ingenuity and fashion sense. It may be possible to cover a damaged part in some way that will not suggest a repair, but that will appear to be part of the styling.

The spot could be covered by a trim, such as braid, ribbon or lace, perhaps taken all round a skirt or bodice, and possibly repeated on a pocket or collar. A design of machine or hand embroidery, or a band of sequins or beads, could be worked across a bodice. An appliqué motif could be used, or even a scatter of motifs. This last can be especially effective with children's clothes, as can deliberately eye-catching patches of bizarre shape or startling colour, on jeans or jackets. The position might be suitable for adding a patch pocket, with another opposite to balance it. Damage to a long sleeve might lead you to cut the garment into a short-sleeved or sleeveless style. Right-side facings or strappings in a contrasting colour or texture can be used to great effect, not only down the centre front but even round armholes, where strain sometimes causes tearing.

The possibilities are endless and their suitability should depend on your own taste. The sketches in *Figure 105a* and *b* may suggest an appropriate idea.

Fig. 105a

Fig. 105b

Panel replacement

Should you have enough matching fabric, it is far better to replace a whole panel of a garment than just to patch it. This is virtually the only way to make a perfect repair on such difficult fabrics as velvet. The existing seamlines would take care of the edges of the panel, and no trace of the repair would show. The suède jacket photographed on page 64 is an example. New seams – placed for instance so as to make a yoke – could reduce the amount of new fabric needed. A separate matching garment such as a waistcoat could even be cannibalized to give enough fabric.

Seaming out

If the garment is generously cut, you may be able to plan a seam or dart to nip out the damage. In this case, a matching seam or dart would be needed on the opposite side of the garment, to balance the new design. This is the best method of all for sheer fabrics, which are usually cut in bouffant styles from which the subtraction of a few centimetres would be of no moment.

Split seams

Repair by Machine

This is the simplest and strongest way to repair a split seam. First, pick out any broken thread ends. Set the same stitch length as for the original seam and stitch on the wrong side along the same seamline. Begin and end six stitches beyond the split. There is no need to tie in thread ends. Press.

It may be that the seam was split in the first place because the garment fitted too tightly; if so, you should consider letting out the side seams at the same time.

The Drawing Stitch

A split seam may not be easily accessible from the wrong side, either because it is in a position where another seam crosses it, such as

at an armhole, or because the garment is lined. In that case, use the tailor's Drawing Stitch, worked from the right side. *Figure 106.*

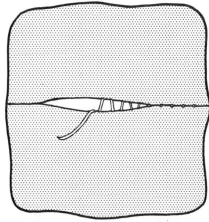

Fig. 106

You will need a heavy thread; on a suit-weight fabric, buttonhole twist is a good choice. Begin with a knot inside the seam turning. Take a small stitch, just along the line of the fold, first on one side and then on the other side of the seam. Begin each stitch opposite the end of the last one, and take a back-stitch at intervals. Pull up rather tightly, and finish off with backstitches. Press with steam.

Hems

A fallen hem should be re-stitched in the same way as it was originally. Thin fabrics are usually turned in and slip-hemmed, as in *Figure 107.* On woollen and other thick fabrics, bias binding or straight seam binding is first stitched to the raw edge, and the binding hemmed to the garment. This avoids the bulk of a turning. *Figure 108.*

In a ready-made garment, the hem will have been worked by machine. The actual stitch used is not built into domestic sewing machines, but the blind-hemming stitch on semi-automatics is a very good substitute. It consists of five straight stitches followed by one stitch swinging to the left. On some machines, there is a stretch version of this stitch for use on knitted fabrics.

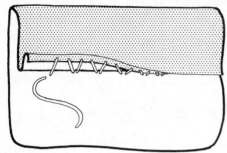

Fig. 107

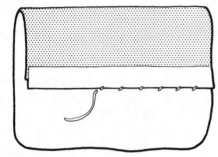

Fig. 108

1. The hem should be tacked in place about 1cm ($\frac{3}{8}$in) from the edge. *Figure 109.*

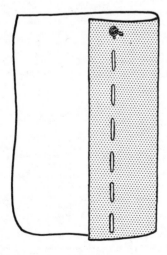

Fig. 109

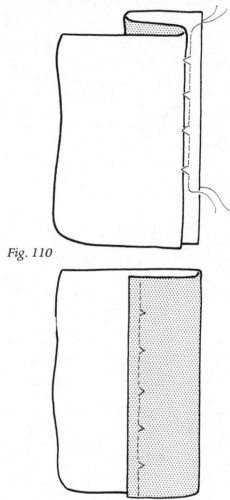

2. Fold the hem back so that only about 5mm ($\frac{1}{4}$in) of the edge projects. *Figure 110.* Stitch along this single thickness, letting only the swing stitch bite into the fold of the garment.

Fig. 110

Fig. 111

This needs to be nicely judged because, if the machining is too far from the fold, the stitches will miss it altogether; if too close, they will leave long threads like exclamation marks on the right side. The blind-hemming foot has an edge-guide that is helpful in maintaining the correct width.

3. The wrong side of the finished hem is shown in *Figure 111.*

Buttonholes

The repair of buttonholes seems to frighten many people who would have no hesitation in working a new one. It is really no different and no more alarming.

The essential first stage is to unpick every single one of the old buttonhole stitches; do not think that you can cobble over them. Leave in place only the reinforcing machine- or back-stitching that may have been laid under the buttonhole stitches.

The buttonhole will have been worked through at least two thicknesses of fabric – the outer layer, the facing and probably an interfacing as well. The new buttonhole should also be worked through all thicknesses, using the same method as originally.

The Dressmaker's Buttonhole
1. Use a heavy, glossy thread such as buttonhole twist.
2. Beginning at the end furthest from the garment's edge and working from left to right, insert the needle behind the buttonhole slit and bring it out at the line of the previous stitching, which you should still be able to see. Or you could work one thread further down if the edges are at all ragged.
3. Loop the thread clockwise behind the eye and under the tip of the needle. *Figure 112.*
4. Pull the needle towards you and upwards, to form the knot along the edge of the cut.

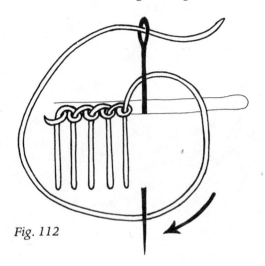

Fig. 112

5. Keeping the stitches close together, work to the right-hand end of the buttonhole. Lay the stitches fanwise round the end – where they have to take the strain of the button. It is sometimes recommended that this end should be whipped or oversewn, to avoid the lumpiness that close-lying buttonhole knots could cause; but oversewing is not as strong, and this is the very point where strength is most needed. It is better to pull the knots up firmly, and settle them closely together with your thumb nail as you work them. *Figure 113.*

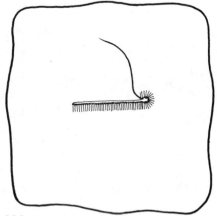

Fig. 113

6. Continue along the remaining side.
7. At the end, slip your needle through the first knot of the other side, to hold the two sides together. Lay two or three satin stitches across the end, and buttonhole over them with the knots lying towards the buttonhole. *Figure 114.*

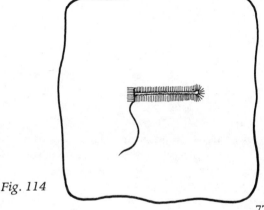

Fig. 114

77

The Tailor's Buttonhole

This is the method used for hand-finishing men's suits; see the second photograph on page 94.

A linen thread should be used on suit- or coat-weight fabric. The stitch is worked from right to left, with the thread wound anti-clockwise under the tip of the needle. *Figure 115*. The stitch is actually a mirror-image of the dressmaker's buttonhole stitch.

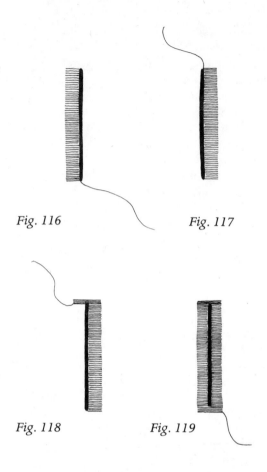

Fig. 116   Fig. 117

Fig. 118   Fig. 119

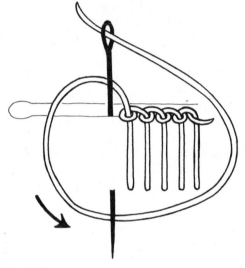

Fig. 115

For extra firmness, lay a thick thread or gimp and stitch over it along the sides and round the end of the buttonhole. Pull up its two ends and cut them off before working the final crossbar.

The Machined Buttonhole

1. Move the machine needle to the left-hand position and set a close satin stitch at half the maximum width.
2. Work along the left-hand side of the buttonhole slit, towards the edge of the garment. At the end, leave the needle down in the fabric at the right-hand side, *Figure 116*, and pivot the buttonhole on the needle. *Figure 117*.

3. Raise the needle, set the widest stitch and work five or six stitches over the same spot, across the end. *Figure 118*.
4. Raise the needle, re-set the narrower width and work the second side and other end as above. *Figure 119*.
5. Pull the thread ends through to the wrong side, knot them and lead them away in a needle between the layers of fabric.

The Bound Buttonhole

A re-bound buttonhole may need to be fractionally larger than the old one.

1. Unpick the old binding from the facing side.
2. Push it through to the right side and unpick the stitching round the slot, to leave the cut shape as shown in *Figure 120*. Press.

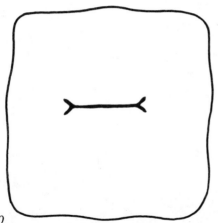

Fig. 120

3. Separate the outside of the garment (and interfacing) from the facing. If the garment is lined, you will have to unpick enough of the lining to give yourself space to work.

4. Cut a patch for the new buttonhole 5cm (2in) deep and 5cm longer than the slot. Tack it to the right side of the slot, matching the straight grain.

5. From the wrong side (where you can see the slot), machine round both sides and both ends of the buttonhole, working a thread or so further from the slot than the original seams. Overlap the ends of the stitching. *Figure 121*.

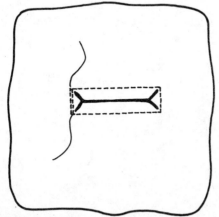

Fig. 121

6. Cut the slot in the new buttonhole patch to correspond with the existing slot, through which you should make the cut, working from the wrong side. Clip into each corner.

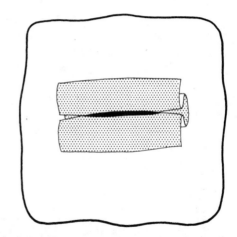

Fig. 122

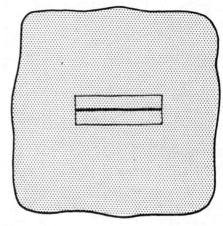

Fig. 123

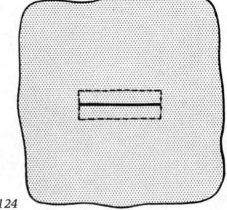

Fig. 124

7. Turn the new binding through the slot to the wrong side, pull the ends sideways and press. *Figure 122.* On the right side, the two lips of the buttonhole should meet in the centre of the slot. *Figure 123.*

8. If extra strength is needed, top-stitch over the four seams from the right side. *Figure 124.*

9. Trim off any surplus binding, to reduce bulk. Fell the facing to the reverse of the buttonhole. *Figure 125.*

1. Unpick a few centimetres of the waistband and cut off the buttonhole end.

2. Cut a new end, using the old one as a pattern and allowing for seam turnings across the waistband.

3. Work the seam and finish the band.

4. Work a new buttonhole. *Figure 127.*

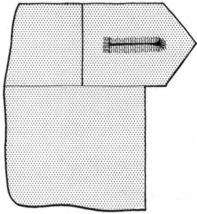

Fig. 127

Darning a Torn Buttonhole

A torn jacket-front buttonhole can be mended by darning on to a backing of tape. This repair is quick, serviceable and strong, but it does tend to show. It would therefore be more suitable for, say, a school blazer than for a good tailored suit.

1. Unpick the stitching of the buttonhole.

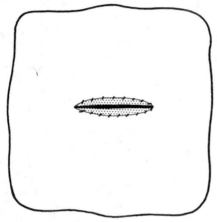

Fig. 125

The Waistband Buttonhole

If the buttonhole at the end of a waistband is torn, as in *Figure 126*, it is best to replace a short length of the band and work a new buttonhole.

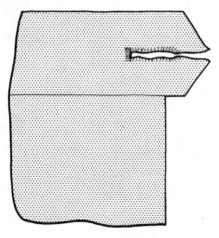

Fig. 126

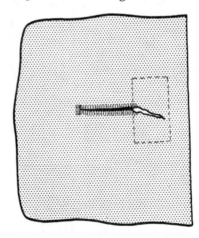

Fig. 128

2. Separate the garment and facing. Insert a piece of tape 3cm (1in) long between the two layers, level with the torn end of the buttonhole, as shown by the dotted line in *Figure 128.*

3. By hand, darn up and down as invisibly as possible, catching in the tape and the facing. *Figure 129.*

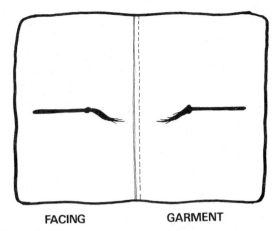

FACING   GARMENT

Fig. 130

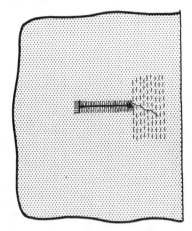

Fig. 129

4. Re-work the buttonhole, preferably by the Tailor's method above.

Patching a Torn Buttonhole
For a really unobtrusive repair, a Tailor's Patch (page 39) is the best method. It will take a great deal more time than the darned buttonhole but, on a good suit, this could be worth your while.

1. Unpick the buttonhole.

2. Unpick the lining down the inner edge of the facing, so that you can separate the garment from its facing at the buttonhole, and work on both from their wrong sides. *Figure 130.*

3. Unpick 10cm (4in) of the centre-front seam opposite the buttonhole.

4. Set Tailor's Patches complete with rantering, as shown on page 39, on both jacket and facing. *Figure 131.* (Work through the fabric *only*; do not take in any interfacing.)

5. Close the centre-front seam, incorporating the outer edge of both patches.

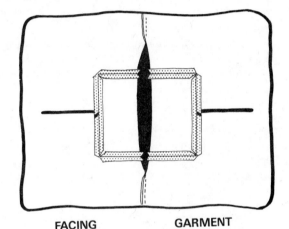

FACING   GARMENT

Fig. 131

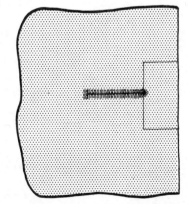

Fig. 132

6. Re-work the buttonhole. *Figure 132.*

7. Re-stitch the lining.

Re-Positioning Buttonholes

If your problem is to work new buttonholes at different intervals, or simply to cover and forget about a row of tattered old ones, then a pair of right-side facings might be the answer. This would be a suitable treatment for the straight front edges of a cardigan-style jacket, but not for a jacket with revers. The existing facings are not affected.

1. First, overcast together the buttonhole slots.
2. For the facings, use a wide petersham (grosgrain) ribbon, or fabric of contrasting texture such as corduroy. Turnings should be pressed to the wrong side – except in the case of petersham (grosgrain), where no turnings would be made.
3. Top-stitch the facing down the centre-front-edge. Then top-stitch the ends and the other edge of the facing. *Figure 133.*

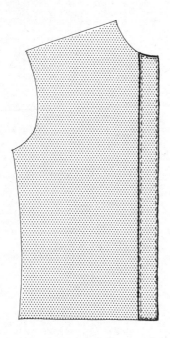

Fig. 133

4. Work new buttonholes at any level, through all thicknesses, and sew on buttons to match.

Buttons

Sew on buttons with linen button-thread, always through two thickness of fabric.

Leave the threads slack enough for the button to stand well up from the garment, so that the buttonhole will not be dimpled down when the garment is fastened. Some people find it a help to slip a match-stick as a temporary wedge under the button, to ensure slackness, but this should not be necessary.

Finish by winding the thread round this thread shank before fastening it off on the wrong side.

If the button has its own solid shank to lift it from the surface of the fabric, then there is no need for a wound thread shank.

Any button subject to much strain should be supported by a small backing button on the wrong side, stitched on as you sew through from the upper button. *Figure 134.*

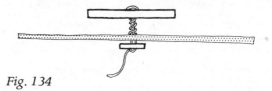

Fig. 134

Zippers (Zips)

Repairing Zips

You may not need to replace a zip that has come apart below the slider. A metal zip (but not a plastic coil-type one) can be re-threaded.

Lever off the end-stop at the bottom and run the slider down to the tape ends below the lowest teeth. Level up the tapes and move the slider upwards. The teeth should then engage. The tapes must now be bound together across the lowest two pairs of teeth; thread a needle with button thread and work six or seven stitches right across, into the tapes at each side. *Figure 135.*

If one tape has lost a tooth from the lowest two or three centimetres (1in or so), the same repair will serve. Remove the end-stop and any teeth below the missing one; level the

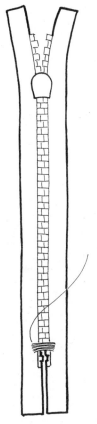

Fig. 135

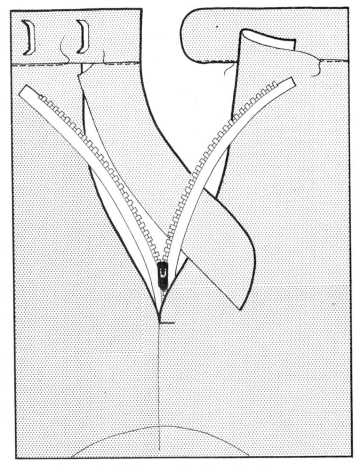

Fig. 136

tapes and push the slider up until it engages both sides. Bind across the lowest two pairs of teeth. You will lose the extra opening length of the undamaged zip, so this repair can only be used where the gap is near the bottom.

A zip that is sticky and hard to move can be eased by rubbing a soft pencil up and down the teeth. For a zip on a light-coloured fabric, talcum powder is an equally effective lubricant.

Replacing Trouser Zips

1. Unpick enough stitching at each end of the waistband to release the top of the zipper tapes. This will also release the left-hand facing and part of the right-hand shield. (The sides will be reversed for women's trousers.) *Figure 136.*

2. Unpick the stitching down both edges of the zip and remove the bar-tack at the end. This will release both the zip and the lower end of the shield.

3. Re-stitch the centre seam up to the bar-tack position.

4. Open the new zip and insert its right-hand tape into the waistband, *under* the trouser front and *over* the shield. Top-stitch the waistband seam. *Figure 137.*

5. Set the zipper-foot on the machine, adjusted to the left of the needle. Machine down the side of the zip, close to the teeth, through trouser front, zip-tape, and shield. One or two pins should be enough to hold the work. The marks of the previous stitching will guide you. Near the lower end of the zip (leaving the needle down in the work) raise the foot and pass the zip slider under it. Work the rest of the seam with the zip closed. Finish off at the level of the bartack. *Figure 138.*

6. Hook the waistband together. Into its left-hand end, insert the left tape of the zip and the top edge of the trouser front. Pin through all thicknesses, and make sure all lies flat. Top-stitch the waistband seam. *Figure 139.*

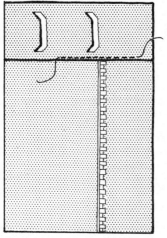

Fig. 137

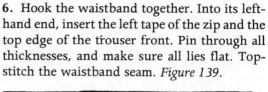
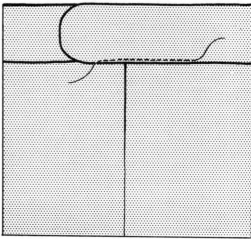

Fig. 139

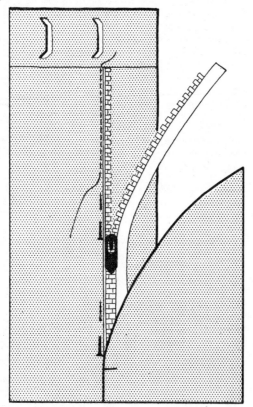

Fig. 138

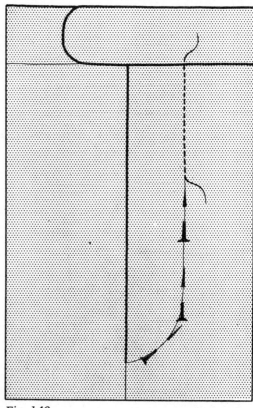

Fig. 140

7. Fold the shield back to the right and pin it out of the way.

8. Pin the left trouser front and facing to the left zipper tape; place the pins along the line of the previous stitching and check that they run down the centre of the tape.

9. Stitch this seam with the zipper-foot set to the right of the needle. You should be able to work the whole seam with the zip closed; if not, leave it open for the first few stitches, then move the slider up before working the rest of the seam. Curve the stitching round the end-stop of the zip, to meet the right-hand seam at the bottom. *Figure 140.*

10. Fold the shield back behind the zip and work a machine bar-tack through all thicknesses – five or six stitches worked backwards and forwards over the same line.

Replacing Skirt Zips

If there is a shield behind the zip, follow the instructions for replacing a trouser zip, reversing right and left for a woman's garment. If there is no shield, just skip the references to it and follow the rest of the instructions.

Replacing Dress Back Zips

The only difficulty in replacing a long back zip by machine is that you will have to work through a tunnel of garment. With a thin, pliable fabric, this is not an obstacle; but it can be awkward on, say, a flannel. So for thicker fabrics you may prefer to re-set the zip by hand with back-stitching. Prick-stitch (the almost invisible form of back-stitch normally used for a hand-set zip) is not suitable where the old stitching lines are clearly indented. The instructions given below for a machined zip are also suitable for a hand-set one.

1. The zipper tapes will have been set into the neckline finish. Unpick the ends of the facings and extract the tapes. Unpick the rest of the zip from the dress. *Figure 141.*

2. With the dress inside out, and setting the longest stitch, machine-baste together the left and right sides of the opening, exactly along their centre-back creases and right down to the seam below the zip placing. *Figure 142.* Press open the turnings.

3. Turn to the right side. Place the new zip under the basted opening. The old stitching lines should still be visible and should be used as a guide for setting the zip. They will show it as having been placed either centrally or to the right side of the opening. Place the new zip in the same position. It is easier to keep a long zip straight and to avoid a serpentine effect if you work from the right side, as you can *see* the stitching lines and *feel* the zip through the fabric.

4. For a *centred* zip, pin as shown in *Figure 143*, taking the pins right under the metal of the zip, at right angles to the seam.

5. Baste where you have pinned, and remove the pins.

6. Fit the zipper foot to the machine. Pull the centre-back hem edge (wrong side up) towards you through the machine until you reach the neckline, and begin with the bulk of the dress on the far side of the machine. Stitch down the centre of one tape; turn; stitch across the lower end; turn and stitch up the centre of the other tape. *Figure 144.*

7. For a zip *set to one side* of the centre-back, it is better to work from the *right* side of the dress, so that you can machine accurately very close to one side of the opening. Then turn, work across the lower end of the tapes, turn again and work the wider margin. *Figure 145.*

8. Remove the two sets of basting and open the zip.

9. Re-stitch the ends of the facings to the neckline, taking in the tops of the zipper-tapes.

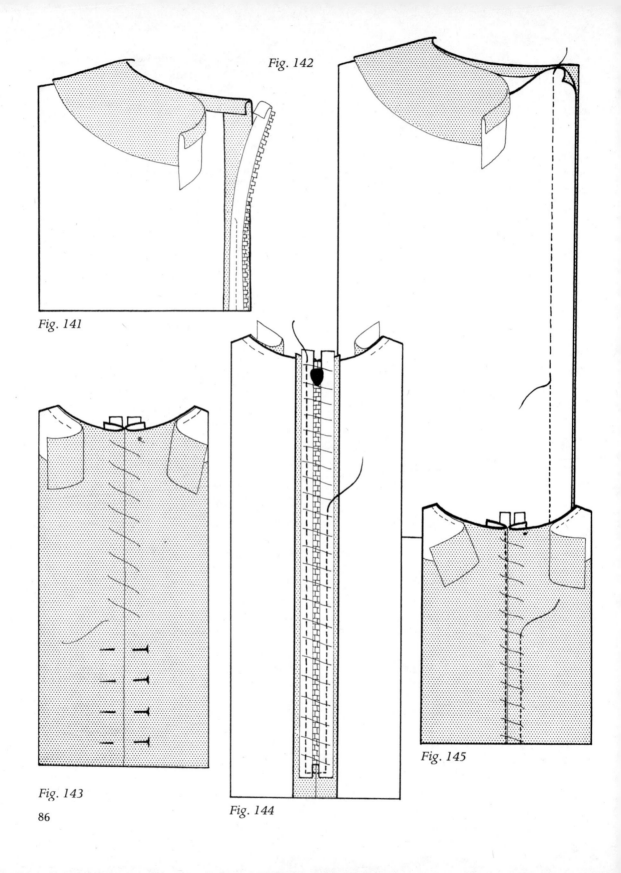

Fig. 142

Fig. 141

Fig. 143

Fig. 144

Fig. 145

Waistbands

Altering

If a waistband has to be altered, it should first be removed entirely. Do not try to lengthen or shorten it at the ends only, as this will throw the garment out of balance.

Usually the seams of the skirt or pants will not need to be altered because of a small alteration to the waistband. There should be enough ease to allow for this; but if not, make the adjustment at the back or at both side seams – not at one side seam only.

To shorten a waistband, cut the surplus measurement from one end. With right sides together, tack the waistband to the garment, evenly distributing the ease. Stitch. Turn the waistband facing to the inside and top-stitch from the right-side exactly over the seam; the top-stitching should sink invisibly into the seam. *Figure 146.*

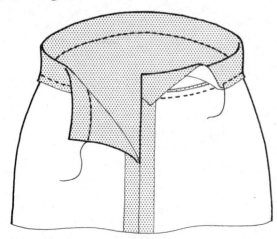

Fig. 146

To lengthen a waistband, insert a strip of fabric either at the centre-back or at the side – whichever avoids the zip placement. Cut the insertion the depth of the waistband and facing, and the length of the extra measurement needed plus 6 cm ($2\frac{1}{2}$in) for the turnings. Apply the same weight and kind of interfacing as in the rest of the band. Work the two seams (*Figure 147*) and apply the band as above.

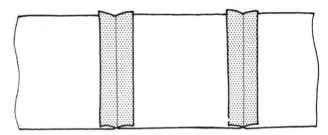

Fig. 147

Replacing with Petersham (Grosgrain)

Should you need fabric for, say, a large patch, the waistband of a skirt or trousers could supply it. Petersham (grosgrain) 3cm ($1\frac{1}{4}$in) wide could then make an invisible finish at the waist.

1. Tack the Petersham (grosgrain) to the wrong side of the garment, with its lower edge to the waist seamline.

2. Top-stitch along this edge from the wrong side. *Figure 148.*

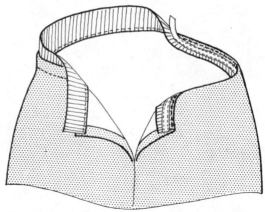

Fig. 148

3. Cover the turnings with narrow seam-binding, stitched to the Petersham (grosgrain) along both edges.

4. Turn the Petersham (grosgrain) to the inside and fasten with a skirt-hook and bar.

Pockets

Replacing a Trouser Pocket

It is a great temptation simply to machine straight across a pocket bag, just above the phalanx of holes at the bottom. If you do this the fabric, weakened already by keys and loose change, may soon give way and you will have your work to do again.

To fit a new pocket bag is not nearly so difficult as it appears at first sight. It is important to use pocketing fabric of cotton, nylon or polyester, which is obtainable in the larger dress fabric stores.

The construction of a side pocket is shown in *Figure 149*. The back of the pocket opening runs down the side seam, from A to B. The front of the opening is set further forward, slanting from C to B. The pocket bag is represented by the dotted line D–E–F. The dotted line from C to B shows the facing inside the *front* edge of the pocket, and the dotted line from G to B shows the facing inside the *back* edge.

length as the old; it will be about 35cm (14in) square.

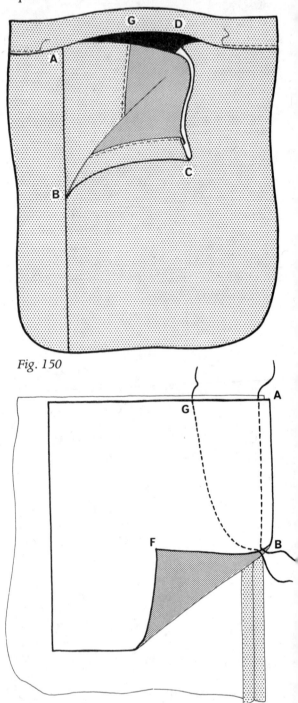

Fig. 150

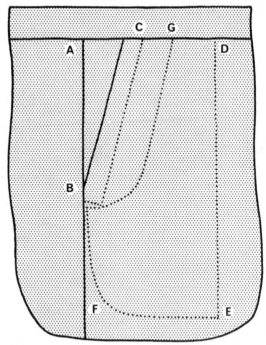

Fig. 149

1. *Figure 150*. Unpick the waistband from A to D, to release the pocket and facings. Cut out the old pocket bag.
2. Cut a new pocket the same width and

Fig. 151

3. *Figure 151.* Turn to the inside of the trousers. Place the pocket piece right side down over the side-seam turning, and stitch from A to B at the bottom of the opening.

4. Turn to the right side. Top-stitch the edge of the facing inside the back edge of the pocket, G–B, over the lining.

5. *Figure 152.* Turn to the wrong side again. Fold over the free side of the pocket (wrong sides together) to match the corners to A and F. The side and bottom of the pocket bag must now be stitched in a French seam. Begin at B, curve round F and finish at E on the fold, Trim this seam.

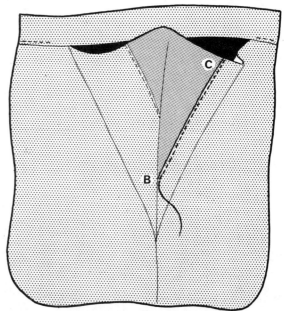

Fig. 153

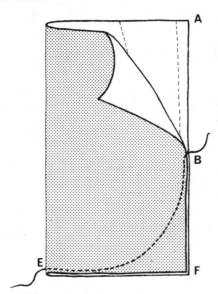

Fig. 152

6. Turn the pocket inside out, press, and work the second side of the French seam 1 cm ($\frac{3}{8}$in) or less from the first stitching, again from B round to E.

7. *Figure 153.* Slip the free side of the pocket bag under the front pocket facing, from C to B, and top-stitch. You may need to trim a little off the pocket edge here, as this is a sloping seam.

8. *Figure 154.* Pin together the pocket opening and slip the upper edges inside the waistband. Tack in place between the waistband and its facing. From the right side, top-stitch from A to D through all the layers.

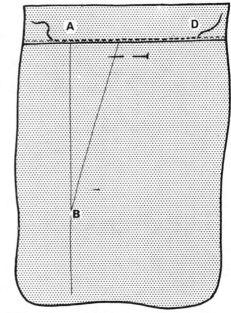

Fig. 154

9. Work a reinforcing bar-tack by machine across the bottom of the opening at B.

Ready-made pocket replacements can be bought, but they are hardly worth the cost, as

89

they will save you only the seam round the bag, and leave you with just as much unpicking and re-stitching.

Replacing a Half-Pocket

This is a much simpler operation. Cut across the pocket bag 3cm (1¼in) below the opening. Unpick 2cm (¾in) up the pocket side seam. *Figure 155.*

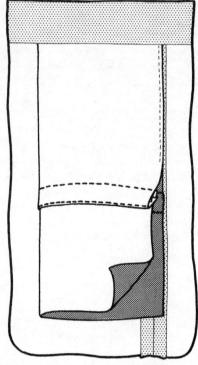

Fig. 156

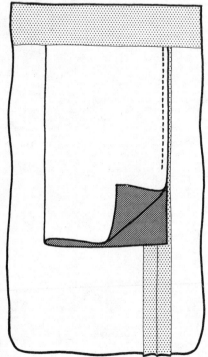

Fig. 155

Cut a piece of pocketing the same size as the discarded part, allowing for turnings at the upper, side and lower edges. With right sides together, stitch the new piece along the lower edge of the pocket. *Figure 156.* On the wrong side, press the seam turnings downwards, trim the under turning to half its width, fold the upper turning over it and stitch.

Close the side seam, curve round the corner and stitch twice along the bottom. *Figure 157.*

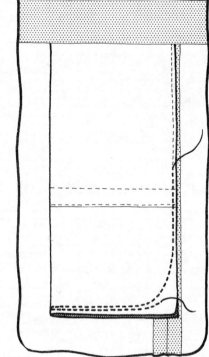

Fig. 157

Repairing a Pocket Edge

Where the edge of a pocket has frayed, as in *Figure 158*, the remedy is to apply a binding, either of tape 2.5cm (1in) wide or of fabric cut on the straight grain.

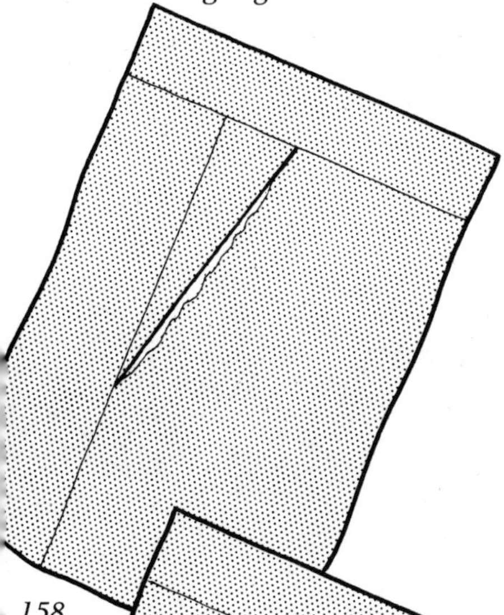

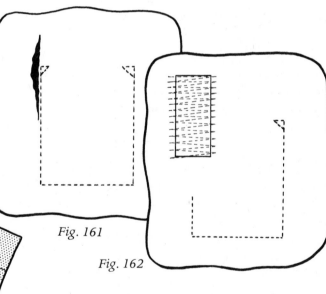

158

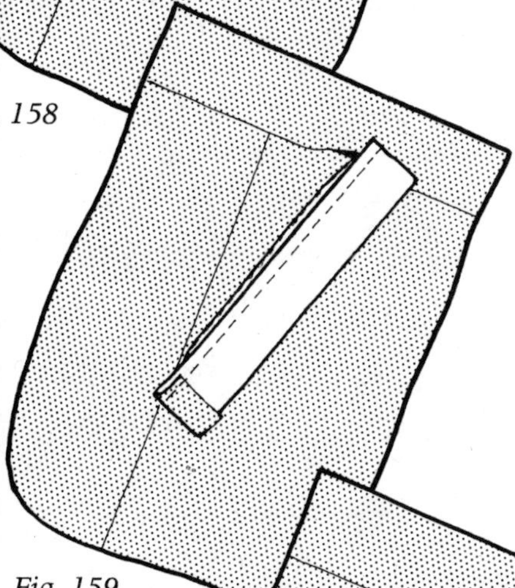

Fig. 159

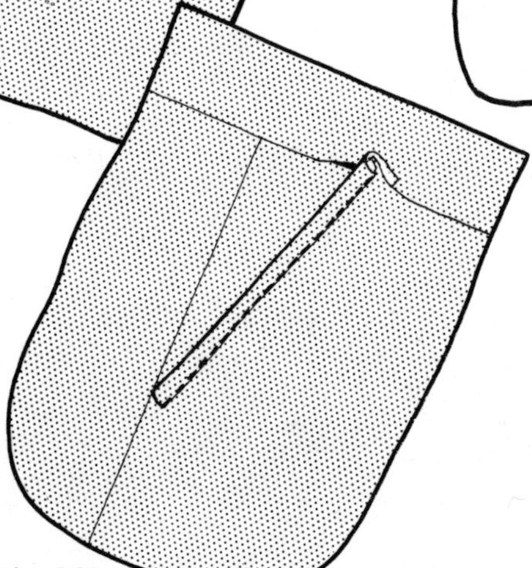

Fig. 160

1. Unpick about 5cm (2in) of the waistband to release the top of the worn edge.
2. Cut the binding 1cm longer than the pocket edge.
3. *Figure 159*. With right sides together, match the edges of pocket and binding. Turn up 1cm of binding at the lower end. Stitch 5mm ($\frac{1}{4}$in) from the edges.
4. Turn the binding over to the inside and press. *Figure 160*. If the turned edge has been machine-finished against fraying, there is no need to make a doubled turning. Top-stitch over the first stitching.
5. Re-stitch the waistband.

Repairing Torn Corners

There are two different ways of working this repair – a very simple one for patch pockets and a formidably difficult tailoring method for slot pockets.

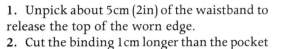

Fig. 161

Fig. 162

a) For a patch pocket

First unpick the corner of the pocket from the garment. You will be left with a straight or triangular tear. *Figure 161*.

Pin a piece of tape (with its ends turned under) to the wrong side of the garment and machine darn the torn edges on to it. *Figure 162*. If the damage is more extensive than can be darned on tape, use instead a scrap of the garment fabric, machine-finished round the edges. Top-stitch the pocket back in place.

b) For a slot pocket

This tailoring repair presents considerable difficulty. Unless you are confident of your skill in working on a small area in an awkward corner, take it to a professional repairer. A whole suit can be made unwearable by such conspicuous damage, so it may be well worth the cost.

The pocket in the photographs on page 93 shows a typical tear, with frayed edges at the pocket flap and piping.

1. Unpick the facing from the lower lip of the pocket, so that you can reach through and work from the wrong side.

2. Unpick the end of the piping and pocket flap far enough to allow you space for the new seam.

3. Cut a patch, bearing in mind the weave pattern. In this case, the patch needed to be three full stripes wide, and was cut from the jacket front facing between the top two buttons, as shown in the third photograph.

4. Apply the patch as shown on page 39. You will need to make five separate seams: bottom, left, top, and lower right sides of the patch, and then the angled seam across the end of the pocket and along its lower lip. *Figure 163* shows the position of the patch; the broken line indicates the piping and pocket flap.

5. As shown in *Figure 164*, work the bottom

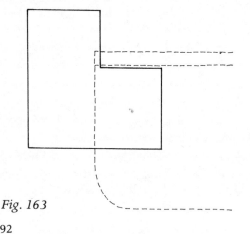

Fig. 163

92

seam of the patch (1) first, to ensure that the stripes are perfectly matched. Then work the left-hand and top seams (2 and 3). (The diagram shows the wrong side, so left and right are reversed.) Lastly, work the lower seam at the right-hand side (4). You will need to trim the patch as shown to allow for the extension below the pocket.

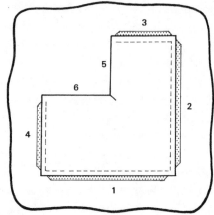

Fig. 164

6. Press the seam edges open on the wrong side.

7. Ranter on the right side of the seams as shown on page 41.

8. Clip into the inside corner of the patch, turn side 5 under, tuck the end of the piping under it and pin through patch, piping and pocket bag. *Figure 165.*

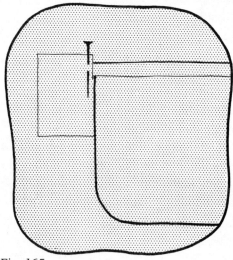

Fig. 165

9. Fell the upper piping and pocket flap back in place, up to the patch. Turn the corner and back-stitch firmly down side 5 to hold the end of the piping and the pocket bag. Lastly, turn under side 6 of the patch and fell it, and the lower lip of the pocket, to the facing.

10. Press with steam under a woollen cloth.

11. With toning fabric, patch the hole in the jacket facing, from which the pocket patch was taken. Re-stitch the lining to the facing.

Jacket front edges

Wear down the front edges, usually at the level of the top button and often exposing the white interfacing, can ruin an otherwise good jacket or indeed a whole suit; so this method of repair can be of great value. It is not unduly difficult, provided that the buttonholes do not have to be repositioned. This depends on the

12 Torn pocket corner on a jacket

13 Tailor's Patch on the same pocket
14 Fabric for the patch removed from the jacket front facing, and replaced by toning fabric

width between them and the edge of the garment; the repair will reduce this stand by 5mm ($\frac{1}{4}$in).

The photographs below show a repair in which the whole length of the seamline was moved inwards. The single buttonhole was unpicked, but could be re-worked in the same position.

Repair to the Edge Only

1. Open up the seam down the front edge from at least 5cm (2in) above the top buttonhole down to the bottom of the facing. *Figure 166*. Also unpick any top-stitching. If the buttonholes are set back far enough to allow you room to work, leave them intact. Otherwise, unpick them completely.

2. Remove the tape stay and trim the worn edge.

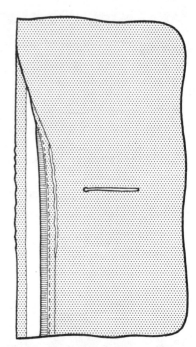

Fig. 166

15 Blazer front edge and buttonhole before repair

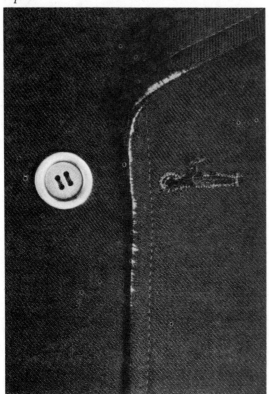

16 The same blazer after repair

3. Stitch a new tape stay to the jacket, working as close to the new edge as is practicable. *Figure 167.*

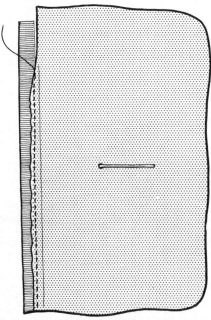

Fig. 167

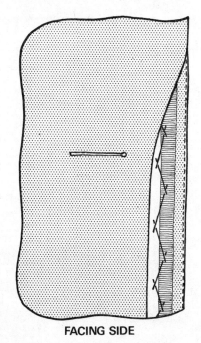

FACING SIDE

Fig. 168

4. Baste and press in the new edge on the jacket, tapering into the old seamline at the upper end. The aim is to achieve a perfectly smooth line. That is why the new seamline should extend to the bottom of the jacket rather than to just below the damaged part.

5. Catch-stitch down the free edge of the stay. *Figure 168.*

6. Trim, baste and press the facing into an exactly matching line.

7. Hand-stitch together the edges of jacket and facing, using the drawing stitch. *Figure 169.* This stitch is shown in detail on page 75.

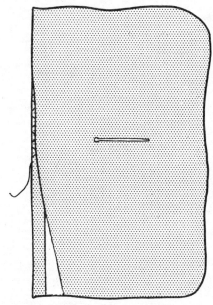

Fig. 169

8. Replace any top-stitching, matching it into the end of the existing stitching.

9. If the buttonhole has been unpicked, re-work it as shown on page 78.

10. Press with steam under a woollen cloth.

Repair with Buttonholes Repositioned

1. Unpick the buttonholes.

2. Unpick the lining from the inner edge of the jacket facing, so that you can work from the wrong side of both jacket and facing.

3. Patch the shank ends of the buttonholes as

shown on page 81, so that they can be moved further from the edge. The patch can be set like the upper one in *Figure 170*; this shows less. Or it can be extended so that the fourth side is taken into the front seam, like the lower buttonhole; this is less difficult to work.

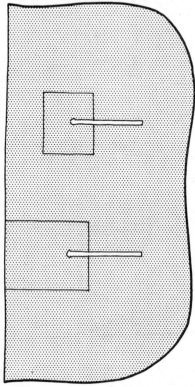

Fig. 170

The garment and facing are patched separately. Unpick the front seam only if it is to accomodate the sides of the patches.

4. Re-work the whole length of the front seam by machine, from the wrong side, setting it back as far as necessary and incorporating a new stay tape. Trim the turnings, turn to the right side and press.

5. Replace any top-stitching.

6. Re-stitch the lining.

7. Following the instructions on page 78, work tailor's buttonholes in the new placings, set back as necessary from their previous positions.

8. Press with steam under a woollen cloth.

Binding with Leather

If you baulk at tackling either of the above repairs, or if the condition of the jacket would not warrant so much work, then a much simpler repair can be made by binding the edge with a strip of leather. It is better to use the grain side, as the suède side very soon looks grubby.

1. Cut the strip at least 2.5cm (1in) wide. It should be long enough to reach from the break

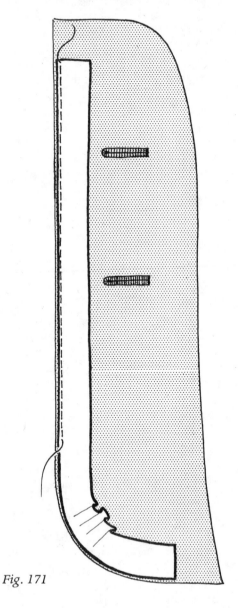

Fig. 171

at the level of the top buttonhole down to the hem; if the jacket front is curved at hem level, then take the binding round the curve.

2. Lay the strip grain side down and level with the jacket edge. *Figure 171*. Set the longest stitch your machine will make and stitch 5mm ($\frac{1}{4}$in) from the edge.

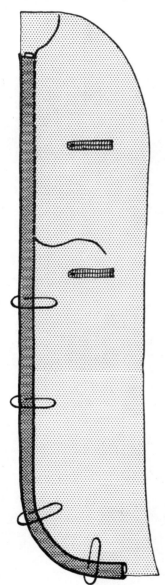

Fig. 172

3. With your fingers, press the leather binding over to the wrong side, but do not fold it a second time as you would with a fabric binding. Then, with a smooth-faced hammer, tap lightly along the seamline and the folded edge; this pounding will flatten the seam and settle the leather into a clean, sharp line. If you choose to press the leather with an iron, it is safe to do so under brown paper, at the setting suitable for wool. **Never use steam on leather.**

4. Hold the binding in place with paper clips. From the right side, stitch exactly along the first seamline, catching in the single thickness of leather underneath. *Figure 172*.

5. Finish the upper and lower ends with a few stab-stitches through all the thicknesses.

Jacket cuffs

Re-Seaming the Cuff Edges

This repair will deal with even the most frayed and ragged cuffs, as shown in the photographs on page 98. It is not difficult to work but it will shorten the sleeve by up to 5mm ($\frac{1}{4}$in); so it may be advisable to see to both cuffs at the same time even if, as usually happens, the left one only has been rubbed threadbare against a watch-strap.

1. Turn the sleeve inside out. Unpick the lining from the cuff facing and push it up the sleeve, out of the way.

2. Cut off the cuff buttons. The buttonholes will probably be worked through one thickness only, so they can be left intact; if worked through both thicknesses, they will need to be unpicked.

3. Take down the whole cuff, including the short seams at the sides of the cuff. *Figure 173*.

4. Press out the crease along the worn edge, and straighten out the interfacing.

5. Turn the facing over to the right side, along the worn edge. Stitch the new cuff seam 5mm ($\frac{1}{4}$in) above the fold. *Figure 174*.

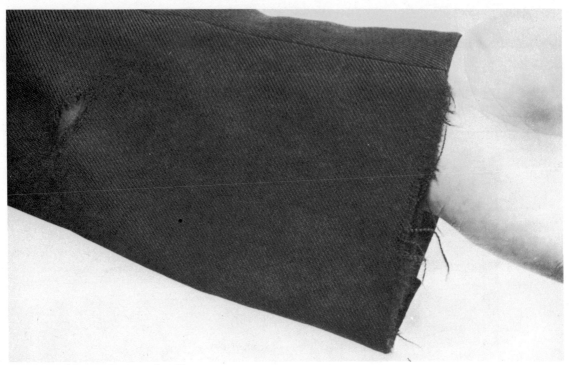

17 Worn blazer sleeve and cuff
18 The same sleeve after repair

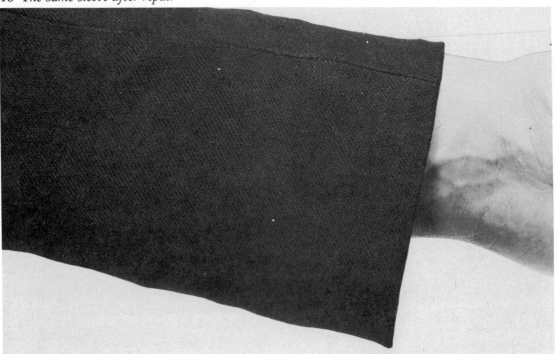

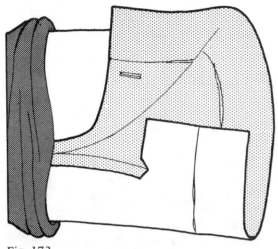

Fig. 173

6. Trim any interfacing from the turning of the new seam. Open the facing out and press it, turning the worn edge downwards. Top-stitch to keep the edge down. *Figure 175*.

7. Turn the facing to the right side again, so that the seam round the cuff falls just to the facing side. Work the short seams at each end of the cuff. *Figure 176*. Trim the corners and turn the facing through to the inside of the sleeve. Both the top-stitching and the cuff seam will now be just inside the new cuff edge. Press with steam under a woollen cloth.

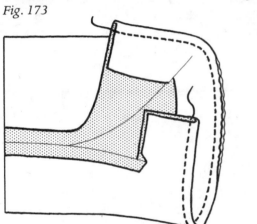

Fig. 174

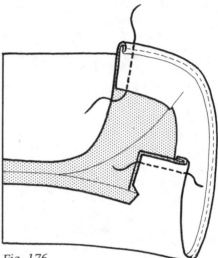

Fig. 176

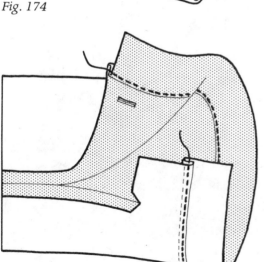

Fig. 175

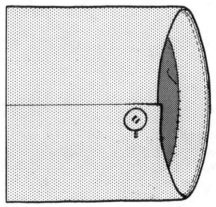

Fig. 177

8. If you have had to open any of the back-arm seam to work the cuff, re-stitch it now. (For clarity, this seam has been shown opened much further than you would actually need.)

9. Re-work the buttonholes, if necessary, as shown on page 78.

10. Lap the front sleeve over the button extension. Sew on the buttons.

11. Re-stitch the lining round the cuff facing. *Figure 177.*

Binding with Leather

This would be a suitable repair for a sports jacket, particularly if the elbows had already been patched with leather. It is much simpler than the repair above. The method is exactly the same as for binding the front edge of a jacket, described on page 96.

You may have to cut off the cuff button to give yourself room to work, but no other preparation is needed.

patches. The narrow cut-like damage along a crease can either be patched with fabric or else it can be seamed out.

Patching with Fabric

The principal difficulty in patching an elbow is one of access. You should first unpick the sleeve lining round the armhole, and then open enough of the back-arm seam to enable you to work on the wrong side of the sleeve. The patch will probably need to be extended to the seam in any case; so that only three sides will be worked, the fourth being taken into the seam.

Use the method shown on page 39. Machine and ranter the three sides of the patch. Re-stitch the sleeve seam from the wrong side, taking in the fourth edge of the patch. *Figure 179.* Fell the lining back round the sleevehead.

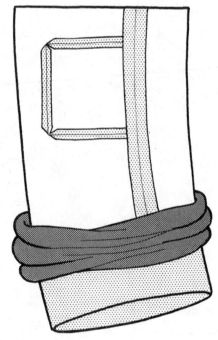

Fig. 179

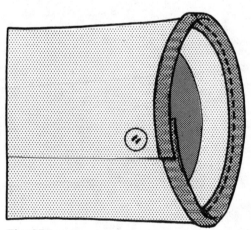

Fig. 178

Elbows

Wear at the elbow of a jacket shows in one of two ways – widely all over the elbow area, or narrowly along a worn crease on the under-sleeve. General wear may cover too large an area to be patched inconspicuously with fabric; then it is better to apply leather elbow

Patching with Leather
1. Use bought patches, or make your own from two pieces of soft leather. These should be shaped like a pair of gibbous moons, to make the patch slightly convex. *Figure 180*. Each piece should be at least 15cm (6in) long by 6cm (2½in) wide.

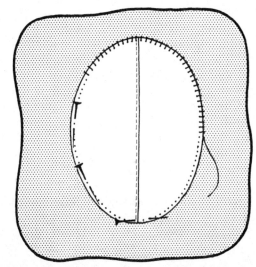

Fig. 181

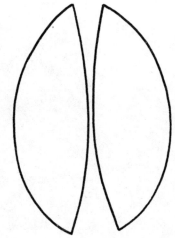

Fig. 180

2. Overlap the pieces and seam them together, using buttonhole twist and the longest stitch your machine will make. An ordinary heavy machine-needle (size 100; US size 16) is perfectly adequate for leather; or you may prefer a special square-section leather needle.
3. Now, with the machine unthreaded, stitch round the patch 3mm (⅛in) from the edge. It will then be easy to stitch through the holes by hand.
4. Unpick a few centimetres down the side seam of the sleeve lining, so that you can get your hand to the wrong side of the sleeve.
5. Pin the leather patch in place and sew it on with buttonhole twist. *Figure 181*.
6. Close the sleeve lining seam by placing the turnings together and machining very close to the folds. *Figure 182*.

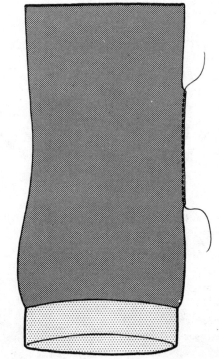

Fig. 182

Seaming a Crease-Cut

Where the fabric has worn through along a crease under the forearm, as in the photographs on page 98, it may be better to repair it with a seam like a narrow dart, rather than to patch it. This is possible only if the amount to be taken out can be less than 1cm ($\frac{3}{8}$in), otherwise the finished sleeve may look wrinkled.

1. Unpick the sleeve lining at the armhole, so that you can work from the wrong side of the sleeve.

2. Stitch the seam as near to the worn edges as you can. Taper to nothing at each end, into sound fabric. *Figure 183.*

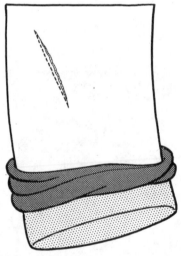

Fig. 183

3. Ranter as shown on page 41.
4. Press with steam.
5. Re-stitch the lining round the armhole.

Trousers

Re-Seating

Trousers often need re-seating before they show wear in other parts. This repair can give extra life even to pants as badly worn as the ones in the photograph. It is a very simple repair to work. If the same colour and

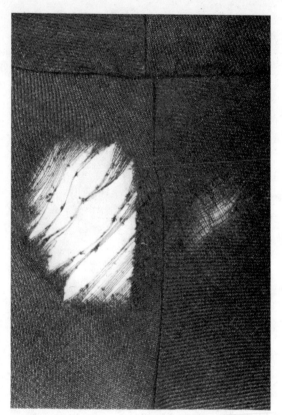

19 Worsted trousers. Seat before patching

brand of trouser is regularly bought, it is as well to keep a worn-out pair as a source of exactly matching patches. Otherwise, a matching waistcoat could perhaps be cannibalized, or a tailor's swatch could provide a similar fabric. But as this repair does not normally show in wear, an exact match is not essential.

1. From the crutch, unpick the innner leg and centre-back seams. *Figure 184.*

2. Mark with chalk the size and shape of the patches needed. It is important that they shold be large enough to cover all the thin areas as well as the holes.

3. Lay the patching fabric under the section to be repaired, if possible matching any weave pattern; but because of the size of these patches you may not be able to match even the straight grain. This does not greatly matter, since there will be a curved side to the patch.

4. Chalk the outline of the trouser edges along

the two sides of the patch. Cut out the patch, allowing for a 1cm (⅜in) turning along the curved side. Press this turning under. *Figure 185.*

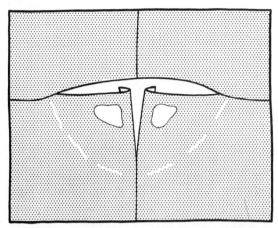

Fig. 184

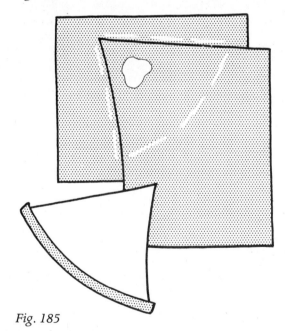

Fig. 185

5. Matching the outer edges, top-stitch the patch to the right side of the trouser section. Then machine-baste the outer edges together. *Figure 186.*

6. Close the centre-back seam, taking in all four thicknesses of fabric – the old trouser

sections and the new patches. The damaged parts are not cut away. *Figure 187.*

7. Close the inner leg seam from one side to the other as a continuous seam. The finished effect is shown in *Figure 188.*

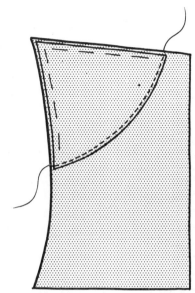

Fig. 186

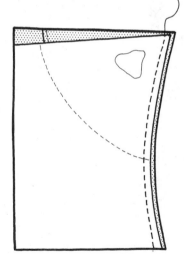

Fig. 187

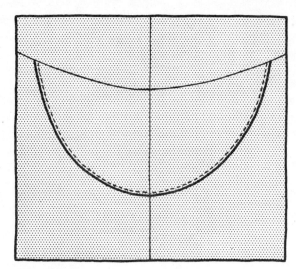

Fig. 188

Darning the Seat

If the damage to the seat is not so extensive as in the photograph on page 102 – if the fabric has just worn threadbare, or into a small hole – then darning is a better solution than patching.

1. The darn must be supported by new fabric on the wrong side. Do not unpick any seams, but fold the pants so that you can mark round the two crutch seams to obtain the shape of the supporting patches. *Figure 189.*

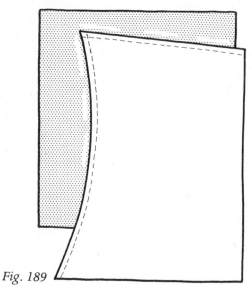

Fig. 189

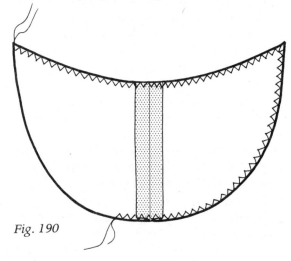

20 *Polyester trousers. Reinforcing patches machine-darned (left) and hand-darned (right)*

2. Cut out the patches, work the centre seam and press. *Figure 190.* Finish the edges with machine zig-zag stitching.

Fig. 190

3. Pin the patch, wrong side down, to the inside of the crutch, matching the seams. Herringbone loosely in place. *Figure 191.*

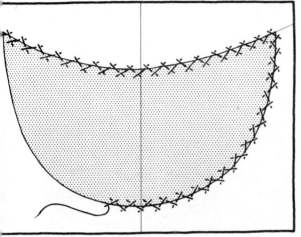

Fig. 191

4. On the right side, darn the hole and thin area through both thicknesses of fabric, either by hand or by machine. For machine darning, set a medium to long stitch and work the rows very closely together, parallel to the seam, as shown at the left-hand side of the photograph on page 104. Unless your machine works a perfect reverse stitch, it is better to turn the darn at the end of each row. This is because the presser-foot on many machines tends to catch the edges of the hole on the return journey. If you have a darning attachment, and can use it without the work being stretched in an embroidery frame, then of course work the darn according to your machine instruction booklet.

5. To darn by hand, work very close rows along the grain (as shown in the right-hand section of the photograph) catching in the supporting fabric behind the darn. Exceptionally, this darn is worked from the right side; so no loops can be left at the ends of rows. If you use a polyester sewing thread, there will be no danger of its shrinking.

6. Press with steam.

Repairing the Hems

Frayed trouser hems can be mended very simply and quite invisibly by either of the methods shown in the photograph on page 106. The leg will be shortened by 5mm ($\frac{1}{4}$in), so it would be as well to make the repair on both legs.

a) with binding

1. Take down the hem.

2. Centre seam-binding over the worn crease and machine along both edges, right round the leg.

3. Turn up the hem so that the edge of the binding falls just inside the trouser bottom. Catch-stitch the hem.

b) with a seam :

1. Take down the hem.

2. Turn it up on the right side, along the frayed line. Work a seam all round, 5mm ($\frac{1}{4}$in) from the fold. *Figure 192.*

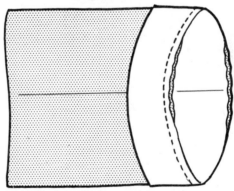

Fig. 192

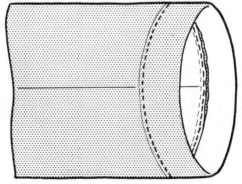

Fig. 193

21 Two methods of repairing worn trouser hems

3. Press the seam turning downwards. Edge-stitch just below the seam, to catch in the turnings. *Figure 193.*

4. Turn up the hem so that the seam falls just within the trouser bottom, and catch-stitch. *Figure 194.*

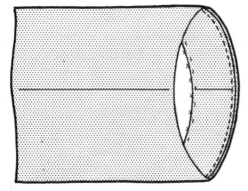

Fig. 194

Dress armholes

Repairing Set-in Sleeves

A worn area at the armhole of a set-in sleeve is repaired in very much the same way as the seat of trousers. Here again, two seams cross each other; they should both be unpicked far enough to let you patch each panel separately. *Figure 195.*

If the patch is to have a curved edge, then apply it with top-stitching to the right side. If it is to have squared corners, apply a tailor's patch (page 39), with rantering on a woollen or thick fabric. Re-stitch the side and sleeve seams before working the armhole seam.

As this repair is likely to show, both armholes should be patched, even if one is still sound. A reinforced darn, as shown for trousers on page 104, might be less obvious. But perhaps the best method is camouflage, such as the armhole facing shown on page 74.

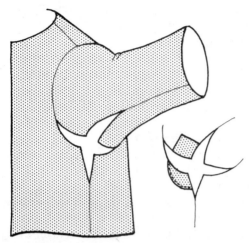

Fig. 195

Repairing Dolman Sleeves

An underarm split in a magyar or dolman sleeve, as in *Figure 196*, must be repaired with a gusset. This will be much less obtrusive than the patches under a set-in sleeve. It will also give more freedom of movement so that the tear is unlikely to be repeated.

Fig. 196

1. Open the underarm seam for 10cm (4in). Trim the sides of the split evenly.

2. Cut a triangular gusset, with its base shaped to fit the line of the underarm seam and its other two sides cut on the straight grain. *Figure 197*.

3. With right sides of garment and gusset together, work an angled seam. Stitch up one side of the split, towards the point. A few

threads above it, pivot the work on the needle and work the second side. *Figure 198*.

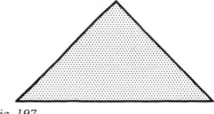

Fig. 197

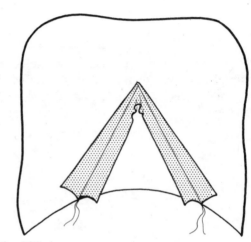

Fig. 198

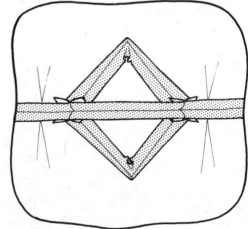

Fig. 199

107

4. Trim the surplus fabric at the point of the gusset. Reinforce the narrow turning at the end of the split with a few buttonhole stitches.

5. Work the gusset on the corresponding half of the sleeve to match.

6. Stitch the underarm seam to take in the curved sides of the gussets. *Figure 199.*

7. Patch the other sleeve to match.

Shirts

Turning a Collar

This renovation is both useful and simple to carry out. It cannot be used when the collar points have a seam on the underside, nor when the under-collar is made of a thinner fabric than the top-collar. Otherwise, there are no snags.

1. Unpick the lowest row of machining inside the collar-band: This will release the edge of the top-collar. *Figure 200.*

2. Unpick the machine stitching that holds the under-collar to the neckline of the shirt.

3. Turn the collar and pin its (old) right side to the right side of the neckline. Machine along the previous stitching; the line of holes should still be visible. *Figure 201.*

4. Top-stitch the edge of the new top-collar inside the neckline, over the previous stitching. *Figure 202.*

5. The buttonhole will now be at the wrong end. Fishbone-stitch its sides together, and sew over it the button from the other end of the collar.

6. Work a machined buttonhole at the left-hand end of the collar, following the instructions on page 78.

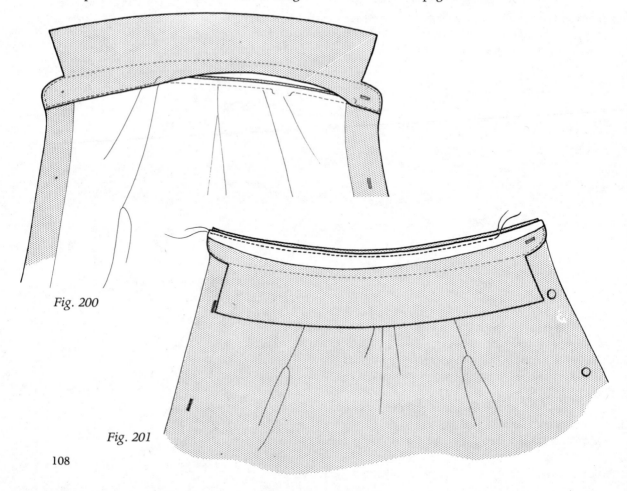

Fig. 200

Fig. 201

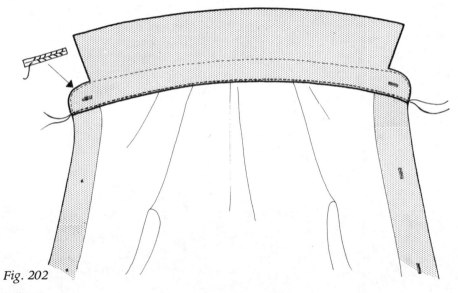

Fig. 202

Turning Cuffs
A doubled-back cuff of the type that fastens
with links can be turned in just the same way
as a collar. The worn edge will then be hidden
inside the fold of the cuff. *Figure 203.*

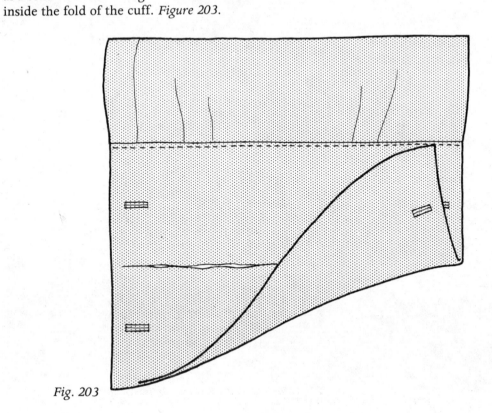

Fig. 203

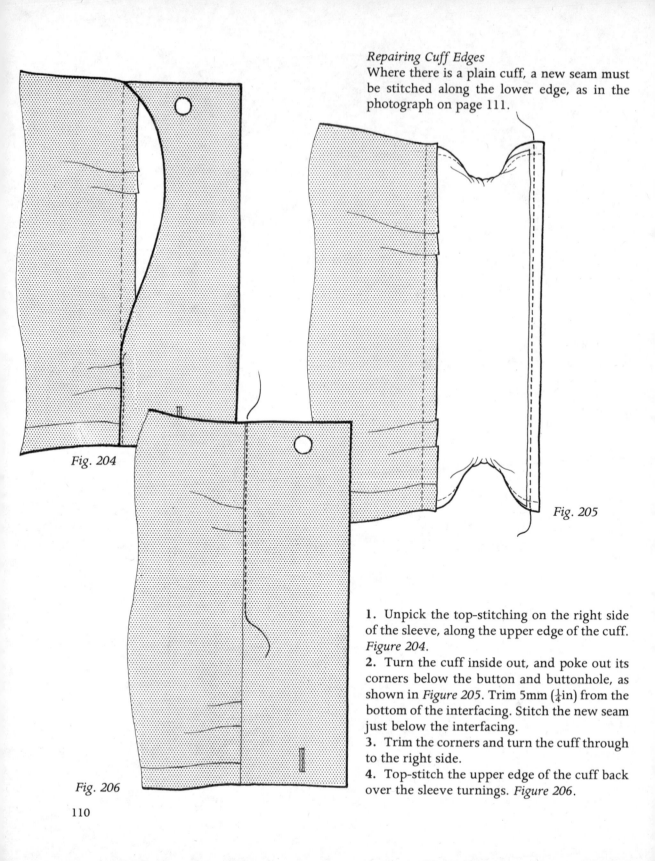

Repairing Cuff Edges
Where there is a plain cuff, a new seam must be stitched along the lower edge, as in the photograph on page 111.

Fig. 204

Fig. 205

Fig. 206

1. Unpick the top-stitching on the right side of the sleeve, along the upper edge of the cuff. *Figure 204*.
2. Turn the cuff inside out, and poke out its corners below the button and buttonhole, as shown in *Figure 205*. Trim 5mm ($\frac{1}{4}$in) from the bottom of the interfacing. Stitch the new seam just below the interfacing.
3. Trim the corners and turn the cuff through to the right side.
4. Top-stitch the upper edge of the cuff back over the sleeve turnings. *Figure 206*.

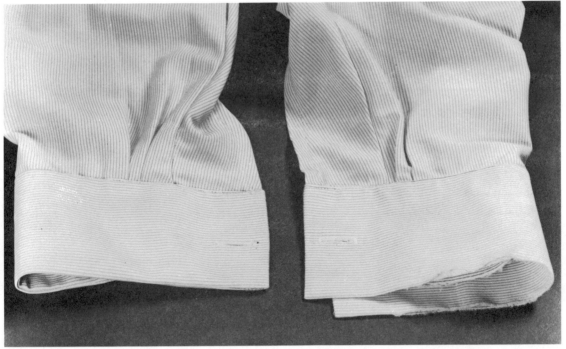

22 Re-seamed shirt cuffs: before and after

Replacing Cuffs

As a last resort, cuffs can be replaced entirely, using fabric cut from the shirt tails.

1. Unpick the cuffs from the sleeves and use them as patterns for the new ones, adding 1cm ($\frac{3}{8}$in) seam allowances all round.

2. Cut out four cuff pieces, one from each front shirt tail and two from the back. Cut two pieces of non-woven interfacing (such as Vilene or Pellon) the same length as the cuff sections but 1cm ($\frac{3}{8}$in) less deep. Along the top of two cuff sections, press the seam allowance down to the wrong side.

3. Slip the interfacing under the folded turning of one cuff piece. Place these over an unfolded cuff facing, right sides together. Figure 207.

4. Stitch through all thicknesses down one end, along the lower edge, and up the other end of the cuff as one continuous seam. Figure 208. Cut off the interfacing close to the stitching along the seam. Trim across the corners. Turn the cuff through to the right side and press.

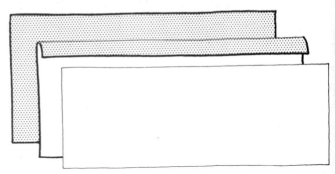

Fig. 207

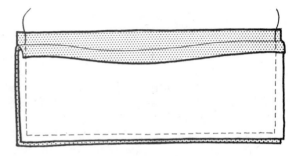

Fig. 208

5. With the top cuff uppermost, work a machine buttonhole as shown on page 78. Sew on the button. Work the other cuff in the same way reversing the positions of button and buttonhole. *Figure 209.*

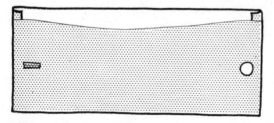

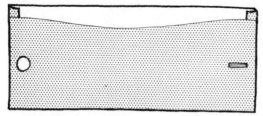

Fig. 209

6. Place the cuff facing to the wrong side of the sleeve, and stitch the seam. (The buttonhole end goes to the overlap edge of the sleeve.) *Figure 210.*

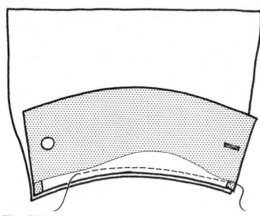

Fig. 210

7. Stitch the top cuff (and interfacing) to the right side of the sleeve, through all thicknesses. *Figure 211.* Top-stitch round the edges of the cuff if liked.

8. Cut the lower edge of the shirt level, press up a narrow hem and machine.

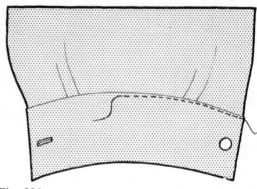

Fig. 211

Underwear

Repairing a Slip
In marked contrast to the fabrics worn before man-made fibres were introduced, modern underwear rarely needs mending before the whole garment needs replacing. Shoulder straps seldom tear the much stronger (though more fragile-looking) fabric of a slip, nor do slips any longer wear thin under the arms.

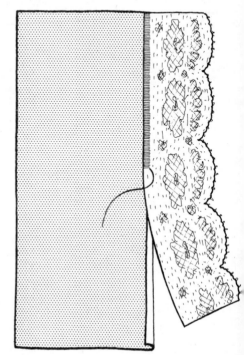

Fig. 212

The most common repair is the replacing of torn lace or broderie anglaise (eyelet embroidery) around a hem. This is the quickest and simplest way.

1. Cut off the old lace and the stitching that held it.

2. Press a very narrow hem turning to the right side.

3. Tack the edge of the lace over this turning. Sew it in place with a machine satin-stitch, setting a close zig-zag of medium width. You will have to try different settings on the fabric to see which looks best. *Figure 212.*

If the lace is to be stitched to the slip along its shaped edge, do not make any turning at the hem. Instead, stitch the lace to the single thickness of fabric, and trim off the surplus on the wrong side. *Figure 213.*

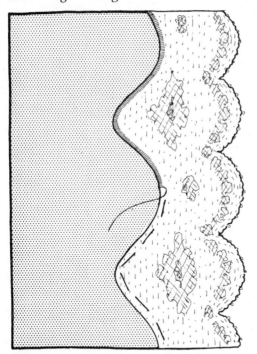

Fig. 213

Broderie anglaise trimming needs to be gathered before setting it on the garment.

1. Work two rows of machine gathering (longest stitch), one 5mm ($\frac{1}{4}$in) and the other 1.5cm ($\frac{5}{8}$in) from the raw edge. Pull up the

threads on the wrong side until the trimming fits the hemline.

2. With right sides together, stitch 1cm from the raw edges. *Figure 214.*

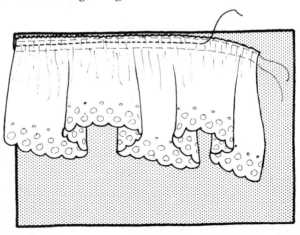

Fig. 214

3. Trim the turnings and finish with zig-zag stitching to overlock the edges together. Press the turning upwards. The seam may be top-stitched if liked. *Figure 215.*

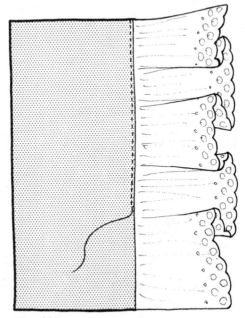

Fig. 215

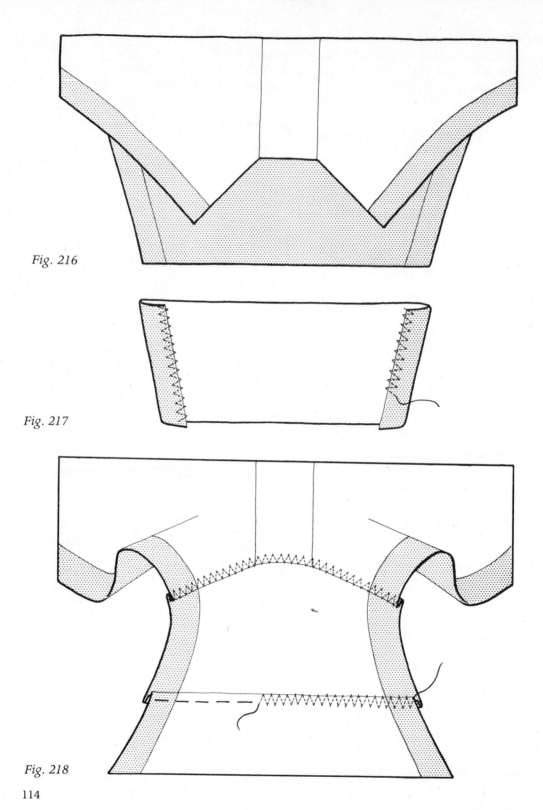

Fig. 216

Fig. 217

Fig. 218

114

Replacing the Crutch of Underpants

The cotton knit fabric used for men's underpants is very stretchable, so any seam used in replacing the crutch piece must be equally so. Use the 3-step zig-zag machine stitch, set at a short length but at its greatest width, as in the photograph. It helps to hold the fabric very slightly stretched as you stitch.

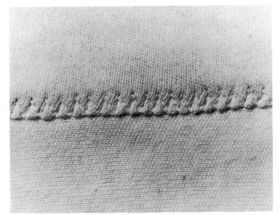

23 Three-step zig-zag seam used to repair stretchable knit fabrics

1. Unpick the seams along the front and back of the crutch section, and remove it completely. *Figure 216.*
2. Use the old crutch section as a pattern for the replacement, which should be cut from an old pair of pants. The wale of the knit should run from side to side of the crutch. Allow for a 1cm ($\frac{3}{8}$in) turning along the front and back edges, and for a 2cm ($\frac{3}{4}$in) hem across each end.
3. Press each hem to the wrong side in a single turning, and stitch over the raw edge. *Figure 217.*
4. Along the front of the crutch piece, press a turning of 1cm ($\frac{3}{8}$in) to the wrong side. Tack the front edge of the pants over this turning, and stitch from the wrong side as shown. *Figure 218.* Repeat for the back seam.

Replacing the Waist Elastic of Underpants

Even for such a straightforward repair, there is a difficult and an easy method. If you begin by cutting off the old elastic, you will have chosen the difficult one. The raw edge of such a stretchable fabric is awkward to set evenly on elastic – so leave the perished elastic in place and let it do the work for you.

1. Use the type of elastic about 2cm ($\frac{3}{4}$in) wide, with a 5mm ($\frac{1}{4}$in) unelasticated selvedge. Overlap the ends and stitch them together using a wide 3-step zig-zag stitch. *Figure 219.*

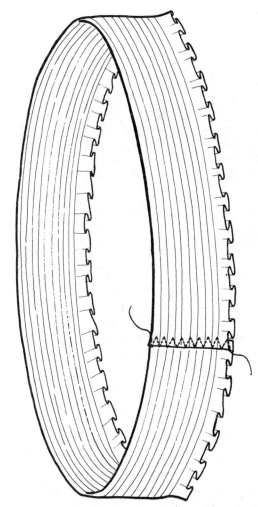

Fig. 219

2. Pin the new elastic as shown in *Figure 220*, so that the selvedge falls well below the existing seamline.

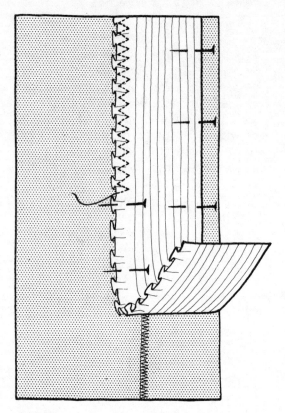

Fig. 220

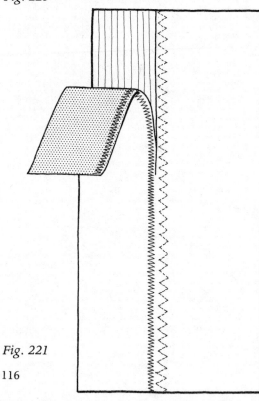

Fig. 221

3. Holding the work very tightly stretched, stitch all round the waistline, along the selvedge.

4. On the wrong side, cut off the old elastic along the top of the stitching. *Figure 221.*

Re-lining

Re-lining a Jacket

When a jacket lining begins to show much wear, it is far better to renew it entirely than to add patch after patch in a proliferating mosaic. Re-lining is not at all a formidable business, except perhaps for the construction of the new inside breast pocket. (If you cannot face that, then a lined patch pocket is a tolerable, though less strong, alternative.)

First, take out the old lining. You will be using the right-hand side as a pattern for the new lining, so unpick that half right down to the last dart. Press the pieces along the grain to restore their original shape. These pattern pieces will be complete with their seam allowances, probably 1cm ($\frac{3}{8}$in) wide, as in the photograph on page 117. The old stitching marks will show the fitting lines and the position of darts.

For lining a man's jacket, you will need about 1.6 metres ($1\frac{3}{4}$ yards) of fabric 140cm (54in) wide. Check this amount by adding together the length of the front, from the neck point to the hem, and the length of the top sleeve. Use the heavy-weight rayon satin lining sold for men's suits; it is a false economy to buy the ordinary tricel or nylon dress-linings as they are too flimsy for this job. The only special care needed in handling the rayon satin lining is the avoidance of any water spots; these will not iron out, so it is advisable to press this fabric with a dry iron.

For the breast pocket lining, you will need 20cm (9ins) of Italian lining – a heavy sateen.

1. Fold the lining right-sides together and lay out the pattern pieces as shown in *Figure 222.*

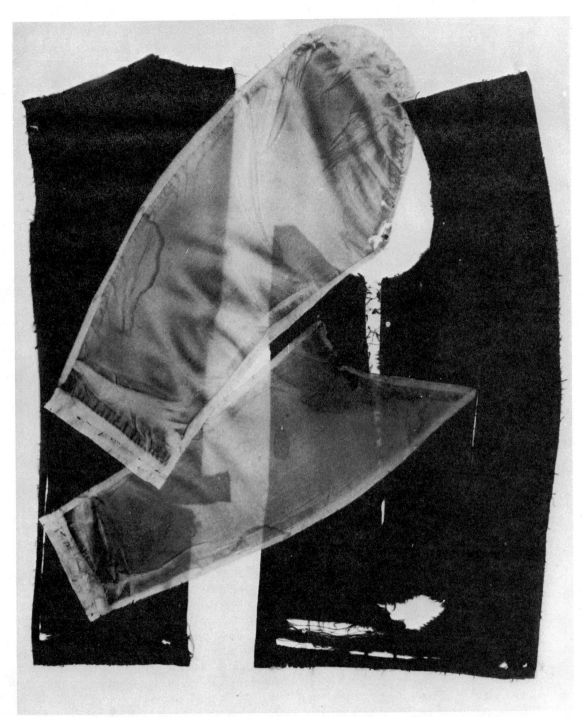

24 *Worn jacket lining to be used as the pattern
for a new lining*

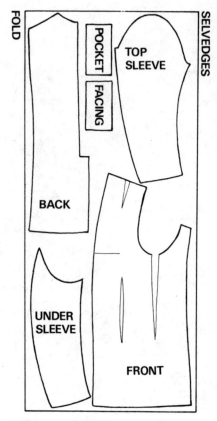

Fig. 222

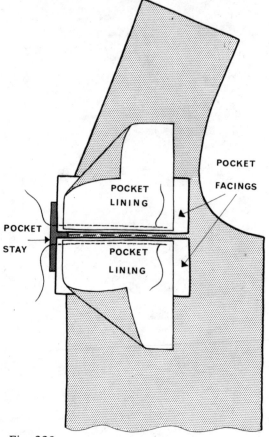

Fig. 223

Cut out. Mark with tailor's chalk or tacks the positions of the darts. On the right front, mark the level and length of the breast pocket opening.

2. First, make the breast pocket. You will need five pocket pieces. From the Italian lining cut:

    1 pocket stay 20 × 5cm (8 × 2in)
    2 pocket linings 20 × 20cm (8 × 8in)

From the jacket lining fabric, cut:

    2 pocket facings 20 × 12cm (8 × 5in)

3. See *Figure 223*. Pin the pocket stay behind the pocket placing. Pin one pocket *facing*, right side down, with its upper edge level with the pocket marking, shown here as a broken line. Pin one pocket *lining*, right side down, over it. The other pocket facing and lining are placed above the marking, with their lower edges meeting it. Machine 5mm ($\frac{1}{4}$in) above and

below the marking, through all thicknesses, as far as the inner end of the mark. Finish by working three stitches back over the previous stitching.

4. *Figure 224*. Cut along the pocket marking, clipping into the corners as shown.

5. *Figure 225*. Turn the linings and facings through to the wrong side and press them into equal lips above and below the slot. Make sure that the triangle at the end of the slot is turned in cleanly. Machine exactly over both seams, from the outer to the inner end of the slot – but not across the inner end.

6. *Figure 226*. Turn to the wrong side. Fold under the free edges of the facings and machine them to the linings.

7. *Figure 227*. Turn to the right side again.

118

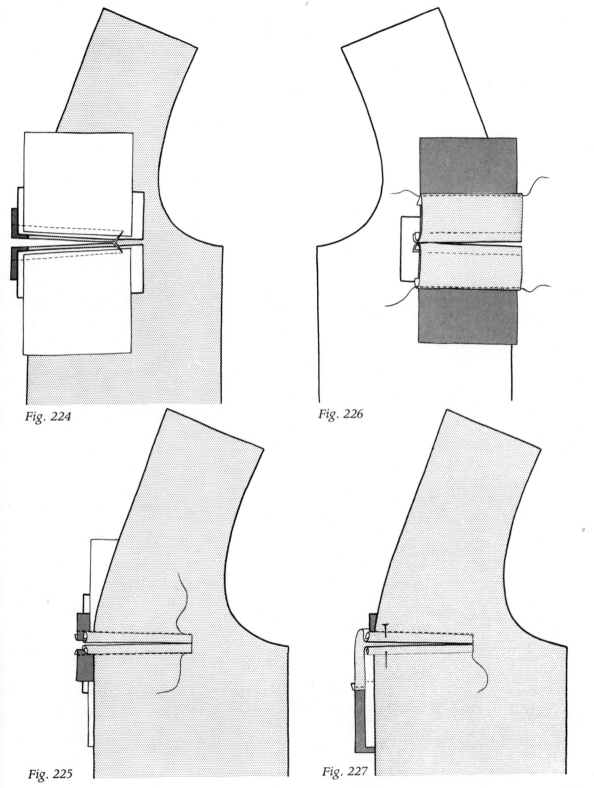

Fig. 224

Fig. 226

Fig. 225

Fig. 227

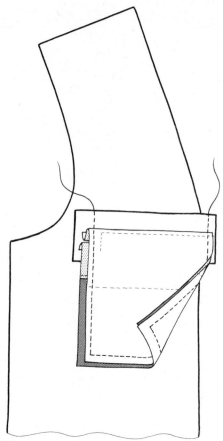

Fig. 228

25 Breast pocket detail of new jacket lining

Press the upper pocket half downwards and pin the two pocket halves together. Machine again along the top edge of the slot and down its inner end.

8. *Figure 228*. On the wrong side, stitch round the three sides of the pocket bag. Trim the turnings. The outer side of the pocket is now ready to be taken into the jacket facing seam, as shown in the photograph on this page.

9. Next, assemble the body lining pieces. Work the darts, centre-back and side seams. Press a pleat for ease down the centre-back, as in the original lining. Do not work the shoulder seams yet.

10. *Figure 229*. Place the jacket and lining right sides together. Machine the jacket facings to the lining fronts, from 5cm (2in) above the hem edge to the shoulder, taking in the unfinished side of the breast pocket.

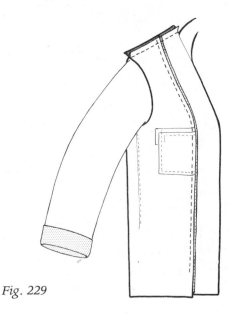

Fig. 229

11. Work the shoulder seams; these will take in the top ends of the jacket facings.

12. Machine the lining to the upper collar along their neck edges, if this is possible. It may be that the collar edge is sewn down securely; if so, it is better to turn the jacket and lining right-side-out, fold in the seam allowance of the lining and fell it in place over the collar neckline, clipping as necessary. *Figure 230.*

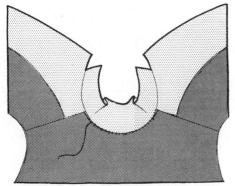

Fig. 230

13. Next, with the jacket and lining right-side-out, work the centre-back vent. *Figure 231.* Turn in and pin the lining to the left edge of the vent, allowing plenty of ease down the centre-back of the lining. Trim the right edge of the lining so that it will lie across the top of the vent. Clip the corner, turn in the seam

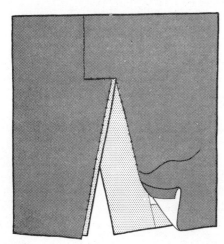

Fig. 231

allowances and pin the lining across the top and down the right side of the vent. Fell in place all round the vent.

14. Now work the lining hem. *Figure 232.* Turn in 1cm ($\frac{3}{8}$in) along the lower edge of the lining. Pin and fell the hem as high as possible along the jacket hem turning, so that the extra ease needed in the lining will form a loose fold.

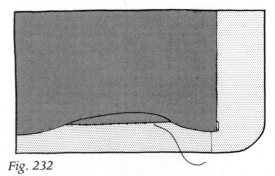

Fig. 232

15. Now make up the sleeve linings. Stitch the top-sleeve to the under-sleeve pieces and press the seams.

16. Match each lining to its sleeve, side by side and inside out. *Figure 233.* Tack together the back-arm seam turnings. This will hold the

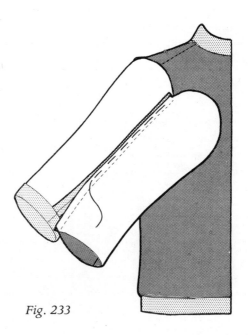

Fig. 233

lining firmly in place inside the sleeve. Now slip your arm down the jacket sleeve, take hold of the wrist ends of both sleeve and lining, and draw them back up through the sleeve. This will bring the lining inside the sleeve, and both will be right-side-out. (The operation is perfectly simple when you have the jacket in your hands.)

17. Finish the cuff ends of the sleeves by turning in the seam allowance and felling, as for the jacket hem. *Figure 234.*

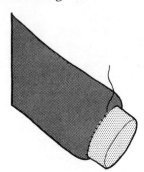

Fig. 234

18. Lastly, finish the sleeveheads. Fold the jacket with the sleeve inside and the lining outside. *Figure 235.* Tack the body lining in place round the armhole. Turn in the seam allowance of the sleeve lining and fell this fold over the body lining.

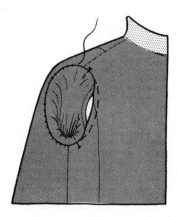

Fig. 235

122

Re-lining a Coat

The only difference between a jacket and a coat lining is that the hem of a coat lining is not attached to the garment, but hangs freely. It is caught with bar-tacks at the seams.

1–12 As for lining a jacket.

13. Turn up and machine the hem to the wrong side of the lining, being sure that it hangs 3cm (1¼in) above the coat hemline.

14. At the side and back seams, attach the lining hem to the coat hem with 1.5cm (⅝in) buttonholed bar-tacks. These will allow some play, while holding the lining down. *Figure 236.*

15–18 As for lining a jacket.

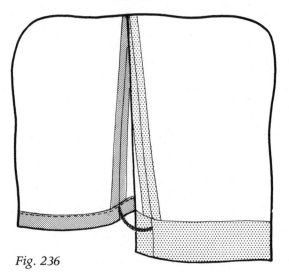

Fig. 236

Re-lining a Skirt

This very simple and worthwhile renovation can greatly improve the hang of a skirt.

1. Unpick and remove the waist finish.

2. Remove the old lining, take it to pieces and use it as a pattern for the new one. If it is distorted, pressing along the straight grain will restore its correct shape.

3. Make up the new lining completely, including the hem.

4. Tack it in place, wrong sides together, round the skirt waistline.

5. Along the opening, fell the turnings to each

side of the zipper tape. *Figure 237.*

6. Re-set the waistband or Petersham (grosgrain), stitching through both the skirt and lining.

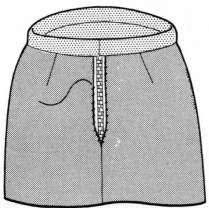

Fig. 237

Glossary

FABRICS

Gauze	Thin, transparent fabric, here used for backing darns.
Herringbone	Weave forming a zig-zag diagonal pattern.
Hopsack	Warp and weft threads woven in groups of two or three.
Interfacing	Fabric used inside a garment for stiffening or strengthening. Fusible interfacing adheres to the outer fabric when ironed on.
Nap	Direction of pattern or surface texture on fabric.
Organdie	Fine, crisp muslin.
Petersham	Thick, ribbed ribbon used for waistbands.
Staflex	Woven fusible interfacing.
Straight grain	The direction of the warp threads, parallel to the fabric's selvedge.
Tarlatan	Stiff muslin of open weave.
Tulle	Fine veiling net, here used for backing darns.
Twill	Fabric woven with surface of diagonal ridges.
Vilene	Non-woven interfacing.
Wale	The direction of knitting, at right angles to the rows. Corresponds to the warp of woven fabric.
Warp, warpwise	The threads along the length of fabric, or their direction parallel to the selvedge.
Weft, weftwise	The threads across the width of fabric, or their direction at right angles to the selvedge.

FIBRES

Acrilan	A form of acrylic. Monsanto trade-name.
Acrylic	A class of man-made fibres, soft and woolly-textured, used mainly for knitwear. Often blended with wool.
Courtelle	A form of acrylic. Courtauld's trade-name.
Crimplene	A crimped form of polyester, used mainly for knitted fabrics. I.C.I. trade-name.
Man-made fibres	Those made entirely from mineral sources. Main classes are acrylic, nylon and polyester.
Natural fibres	Those taken from animal or vegetable sources: cotton, linen, silk, wool.
Nylon	Polyamide, the first man-made fibre.
Polyester	A class of man-made fibres, smooth-surfaced, used for woven or knitted fabrics. Often blended with cotton etc.

Rayon	The first synthetic fibre, made from wood-pulp.
Synthetic fibres	Term loosely used for fibres made wholly or partly from natural cellulose, such as rayon or tricel.
Terylene	Form of polyester. I.C.I. trade-name.
Tricel	Synthetic fibre resembling silk. Courtauld's trade-name.

MACHINES

Bobbin thread	The lower thread in a sewing machine.
Darning foot	Machine presser foot used for darning or embroidery when the fabric is moved by hand and not by the feed-dog.
Feed-dog	Toothed mechanism that draws the fabric through the sewing machine.
Leavers machine	Industrial machine for making bobbin lace.
Needleplate	The metal plate over which the fabric passes through the machine.
Needle thread	The upper thread in a sewing machine.
Presser foot	The part that applies pressure to the fabric under the machine needle.
Schiffli machine	Industrial machine for making needlepoint lace or for embroidering.
Swing-needle machine	Sewing machine which can be set to produce zig-zag stitching, alternately to the left and right.
Zipper foot	Presser foot which allows the needle to stitch close to the teeth of a zip-fastener.

NEEDLES AND THREADS

Ball-point needle	Rounded tip, for machining fine jersey.
Buttonhole twist	Heavy, glossy thread for hand-worked buttonholes.
Button thread	Heavy thread, usually linen, for sewing on buttons.
Crewel needle	Has long, narrow eye for embroidery threads.
Darning needle	Long needle with long eye for darning threads.
Gloving needle	Spear-pointed needle for sewing leather by hand.
Latch-needle	Small hook set in a handle, used for re-weaving the sides of patches.
Leather needle	Spear-pointed, for machining leather.
Polyester thread	Stronger than cotton thread, for use on all man-made fibres.
Tapestry needle	Blunt-pointed, to pass through fabric without splitting the threads. Large eye.

STITCHES AND PROCESSES

Bar-tack	*By machine:* long stitches to reinforce the end of an opening. *By hand:* buttonholed bar to hold lining to coat hem etc.
Basting	Temporary stitching to hold work until it is pressed or permanently stitched.
Blind-hemming	Invisible hemming stitch worked on swing-needle machines. *Figure 110.*
Couching	Stitching to hold down a thread laid on the surface of the fabric. *Figure 86.*
Herringboning	Stitches crossing over alternately above and below the edge of a hem or patch. *Figure 37.*

126

Mitring	Trimming fabric from the angle of a seam, to reduce bulk.
Rantering	Methods of strengthening or camouflaging the edges of a patch.
Re-weaving	Various forms of invisible mending.
Satin stitching	Wide, closely-set zig-zag machine stitching.
Stretch-stitching	On automatic machines, a stitch pattern including a reverse stitch, for sewing knitted fabrics.
Tacking	Temporary stitching to hold the work until it is permanently stitched.
Three-step zig-zag	On swing-needle machines, a stitch pattern made in threes, alternately to right and left.
Top-stitching	Machine stitching worked from, and visible on, the right side of the fabric.
Zig-zag stitching	On swing-needle machines, stitches made alternately to right and left.

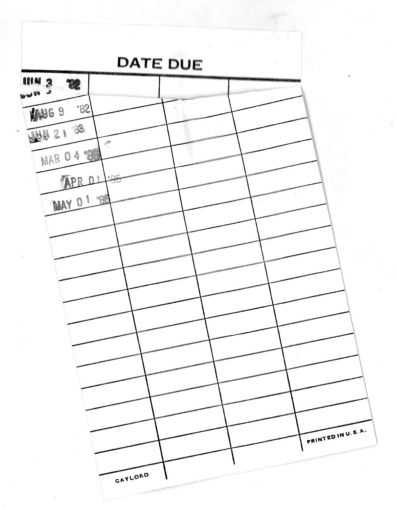

DATE DUE

JUN 3 '82			
AUG 9 '82			
JUN 21 '83			
MAR 04 '85			
APR 01 '95			
MAY 01 '96			
			PRINTED IN U.S.A.

GAYLORD